T0066839

JeANNie

OUT of

THe

BoTTLe

BARBARA EDEN

＊ ＊ ＊ ＊ *with Wendy Leigh* ＊ ＊ ＊ ＊

JeANNie
OUT of
THe
BoTTLe

＊ ＊ ＊ ＊ ＊ ＊ ＊ ＊ ＊ ＊ ＊ ＊ ＊ ＊

Three Rivers Press
New York

Originally published in hardcover in the United States by Crown Archetype, an imprint
of the Crown Publishing Group, a division of Random House, Inc., New York, in 2011.

Library of Congress Cataloging-in-Publication Data

Eden, Barbara, 1934–
Jeannie out of the bottle / Barbara Eden with Wendy Leigh.—1st ed.
p. cm.
1. Eden, Barbara, 1934–   2. Television actors and actresses—
United States—Biography.   I. Leigh, Wendy.   II. Title.
PN2287.E384A3 2011
791.45'028'0924—dc22
[B]   2011001058

ISBN 978-0-307-88696-5
eISBN 978-0-307-88695-8

Cover design by Laura Duffy
Cover photograph: NBC/Photofest

First Paperback Edition

146122990

For my loving husband, Jon,

my devoted manager, Gene Schwam,

and of course Sidney Sheldon.

CONTENTS

CONTENTS

JeANNie

OUT of

THe

BoTTLe

INTRODUCTION

December 1, 1964, Sunset Boulevard, Los Angeles, California

It's the end of the first day filming the *I Dream of Jeannie* pilot, "The Lady in the Bottle," and three of us—the series's creator, writer, and producer, Sidney Sheldon; Larry Hagman, who plays Captain Anthony Nelson; and I—are in the company limo speeding the thirty miles from Malibu back to Hollywood after a long day on location at Zuma Beach, the scene of Captain Nelson's first meeting with Jeannie.

Still in my flimsy pink chiffon harem-style pantaloons and minuscule velvet bolero, I shiver from head to foot, snuggle into my brown cloth coat, and wish I'd been allowed to keep my full-length mink from my days as Loco in the TV series *How to Marry a Millionaire.*

How to Marry a Millionaire ran for two years, but—although I'm happy to be playing Jeannie, and thrilled that my first day went so well—I'm not counting on the *I Dream of Jeannie* pilot being sold at all. But it's a job, and I'm glad to have gotten it, though I'm still stunned that Sidney Sheldon didn't cast a tall, willowy, raven-haired Middle Eastern beauty queen as his Jeannie instead of a short American blonde like me.

The limo glides to a halt at a traffic light, right next to a maroon Mustang convertible sporting Kansas license plates and driven by an elderly man and his middle-aged wife.

Without any warning, Larry rolls down the limo window, leans out, and to my utter amazement yells at the couple, "Someday I'm going to be a star! Someday you're going to know who I am!"

When I recover from my surprise, I think, *A star! Why in the blazes would he—or anyone else, for that matter—ever want to be a star?*

I blink my Jeannie-style blink and flash back two years to April 10, 1962, on the sound stage at Twentieth Century Fox, where I am filming *Five Weeks in a Balloon* with Red Buttons, and Marilyn Monroe is filming *Something's Got to Give* on sound stage 14, which is adjacent to mine. Evie—Evelyn Moriarty, my stand-in since I first arrived at Fox in 1957, and Marilyn's as well—announces in her inimitable twang, "Barbara, my other star has asked to meet you!"

I know she means Marilyn Monroe, because that's how she always refers to her, and I am both thrilled and curious to meet Marilyn at last. After all, Evie has been confiding in me about her for years. So although I am dressed for the movie like a clown in baggy plaid pants and a massive white shirt, when Evie grabs my hand and pulls me over to the *Something's Got to Give* sound stage, where Marilyn is about to start a wardrobe test, I follow her without a moment's hesitation.

Fox sound stages in those days were huge, like small cities, and this one is a massive cavern, with a little lighted circle in the middle. A trailer in the background serves as Marilyn's dressing room, where the legendary costume designer Jean Louis is working with her on her wardrobe for *Something's Got to Give* as well as the sensational figure-hugging gown she will soon be wearing when she sings "Happy Birthday" to President Kennedy at Madison Square Garden.

But, of course, none of us knows any of that yet. Nor do we have a glimmer that *Something's Got to Give* will be Marilyn's final movie. Had we known what lay ahead for her, we would have been shocked to the core.

Then the trailer door opens, and Marilyn materializes on the set. Evie grabs my hand and utters the immortal line, "Marilyn, I want you to meet my other star. . . ."

My other star—that's how Evie describes *me,* the former Barbara Jean Huffman, to Marilyn Monroe!

I step into the spotlight with Marilyn. She takes my hand. We have a conversation, during which I try to put everything Evie has revealed to me about Marilyn firmly out of my mind (I'll tell you more later) and instead do my utmost to focus on this vision of loveliness in front of me.

So I'm standing there, the image of Bozo the Clown on a bad day, but Marilyn is the most beautiful thing I've ever seen in my life. She just glows. There is something in the ether swirling about her, in her, through her, around her, and if James Cameron, the director of *Avatar,* had seen her, he'd have cast her as one of his special people. She's every inch a star, but after what Evie has confided to me, I don't envy Marilyn, not an iota.

And I don't envy any of the other stars I've met and worked with up till now, either. None of them, not Elvis Presley (who tried to seduce me by confiding his vulnerabilities to me), not Paul Newman (who, strangely enough, had a complex about his physical appearance), not Lucille Ball (who was forced to cope with her husband's very public infidelity on practically a daily basis). Stars each and every one of them. But happy and fulfilled? I wonder.

As for me, right now I'm an actress, not a star, and I'm content with that. But here in the limousine speeding back to Hollywood after the first day of filming the *I Dream of Jeannie* pilot is Larry Hagman, clearly burning with red-hot ambition to become a star, and, more important, passionately believing that *I Dream of Jeannie* will instantly make him one.

This is what Sidney Sheldon said many years later about Larry's unbridled ambition: "Suddenly, Larry found himself in a show with a beautiful half-naked girl and there was no way that it would be *his* show. I tried everything, but it was always only Jeannie the public was interested in, and through five seasons he became frustrated and very angry."

On a good day, I understood and sympathized with Larry's frustration and anger. On a bad day . . . well, I'll tell you about those bad days, and you can judge for yourselves. First, though, another Jeannie blink.

It's 1938 and I'm at school in San Francisco. I'm one of the poorest children in the school, and certainly not one of the prettiest. I may be proud of my school shoes (the only other pair I own are church shoes), but I'm not in the least bit crazy about the pigtails my mom wants me to wear all the time because she thinks they look cute.

My mother is so proud of those pigtails that I never once complain when she braids them tightly every morning. Today, at the end of class, a couple of the boys have fun pulling them over and over again real hard—maybe because they don't like me, maybe because they like me too much and are trying to get my attention. I don't really know. All I do know is that they are hurting me a lot.

As soon as I can, I yank myself away and run home in floods of tears. My mother takes one look at me and declares, "Rise above it, Barbara Jean! Rise above it!" And I think, *Rise above it? Rise above it? I'm only four years old. How the heck can I rise above anything?*

But I love and trust my mother, so I dry my tears, try to rise above my bullying schoolmates, and, by some kind of a miracle, actually succeed. From that time on, my mother's early decree to "rise above it" will become indelibly engraved on my psyche. It will become my own private mantra, the way I live my life and cope with whatever fate will throw at me through the years—through all the hungry years of the late fifties and early sixties when I was a struggling Hollywood contract player, through the bitter weeks of trying to survive as a chorus girl at Ciro's supper club, through the hairy moments as Johnny Carson's comic sidekick on live TV, through my days on *I Love Lucy* doing my utmost to avoid Desi Arnaz's sexual advances, through my heart-pounding on-screen cameo with Paul Newman, and through my weeks as Elvis Presley's leading lady, spending hours drinking in his vulnerable sweetness, only to discover years later that he secretly had amorous designs on me as well.

My mother's edict stayed with me through all my years of tangling with Hollywood's most high-testosterone players: Warren Beatty, Burl Ives, Tom Jones, Tony Randall, Tony Curtis, O. J. Simpson, and more. And through all the lonely years when—on the verge of a breakdown after my younger son was stillborn—I performed in Las Vegas, shared George Burns's dressing room, and smiled through my tears as best I could.

Most of all, her words echoed in my mind during those five seasons of working with Larry Hagman on *I Dream of Jeannie,* which sometimes felt like I was walking on hot coals. But before I tell you about some of the most challenging moments, I want to make it crystal clear that I think Larry Hagman is a terrific actor and I'd work with him again any day, not just because of his talent but because he is a warm and kind human being.

Let me Jeannie-blink an example for you. We have a guest director on the show, whose name I have mercifully blanked out simply because the memory of him is so unpleasant. He is an old-time movie director, the relative of some studio bigwig. He is long past his prime as a director and probably should have retired, because he is now borderline senile.

As it is, he is extremely frustrating to work with because he doesn't always make himself clear when he sets up a scene, so that none of us knows where we are supposed to stand or what we are supposed to do. The end result is that we work long hours in the studio without getting much film in the can. One day a situation ensues that goes something like this:

CAMERAMAN: "Cut!"

DIRECTOR: "Who said cut?"

CAMERAMAN: "I did, sir!"

DIRECTOR: "Why did you say cut? You're not supposed to say cut!"

CAMERAMAN: "I said cut because someone walked in front of the camera, sir."

DIRECTOR: "Who did that? Who did that? Whoever did that, they're fired!"

CAMERAMAN: "But that was you, sir!"

(I suppose that *I Dream of Jeannie* director was a minor improvement over director Irwin Allen, with whom I worked on a couple of movies, although at the time I didn't quite see it that way. Irwin wasn't senile, just wildly eccentric, and imagined that he was Cecil B. DeMille. Instead of yelling "cut," he would fire a gun into the air.)

Toward the end of a day of working on *I Dream of Jeannie* with that senile, tyrannical old movie director barking ludicrous orders at us incessantly, I am close to tears. So, during a short break in the filming, I run off the set and hide behind a piece of scenery, far removed from all the action. And I stay there, sobbing away as silently as possible, while my makeup pours down my cheeks and all the crew and cast run around trying to find me.

Of course, Larry, a clever man in all sorts of ways, is the one to finally find me in my hiding place. He puts his arms around me gently and says, "Don't cry, Barbara. That's my act!" Bless his heart! I am simultaneously touched and surprised—touched that Larry is being so kind to me, and surprised that he is being so honest about his on-set emotional breakdowns, which sometimes actually did culminate in him crying in front of all of us.

But *I Dream of Jeannie* wasn't just a hotbed of drama and intrigue. It was also a comedy, and Larry and I had plenty of fun along the way as well. A classic Larry story involves the two of us and a lion named Simm, a veteran of *The Addams Family*, who appeared with us in an episode entitled "The Americanization of Jeannie."

The plot has Jeannie begging Captain Nelson to allow her to bring her former pet into the house. Not knowing what kind of pet Jeannie means, he agrees, only to be confronted with a fully grown male African lion.

Let me Jeannie-blink back to what really happened behind the scenes. As chance would have it, I've worked with lions before on a couple of Fox movies, and now I consider myself somewhat of a lion expert. So before we shoot our scene with the lion, I take Larry aside, advise him to make friends with the lion, and explain how.

"Here's what you do, Larry. You have to stand very still and let the lion smell you. Then, when he's finished doing that, you should lean forward very, very gingerly and stroke him as gently as you can. That way, he'll get to know you and everything will be fine," I say helpfully.

Larry's reaction? "Dream on, Barbara. I'm not making friends with any f—— lion!" He strides back to his dressing room.

At that moment, the lion trainer leads the lion onto the set. Larry and I were supposed to sit on the couch, and at a certain point in the script the lion was meant to stick his big paws over the back of the couch.

While the scene is being set up and the props put in place, I go through my routine of bonding with the lion. I let him smell my fingers and lick my hand, then slowly, very slowly, I stroke him under his chin. He gives me a sidelong glance and visibly relaxes, and I silently congratulate myself on our new and warm friendship.

The lion is led away from the couch. After a few minutes, Larry walks back onto the set and sits down next to me, while the director places a piece of raw meat between us. The lion is led right up to the couch, takes one look at Larry, and lets out an almighty roar. Whereupon Larry bolts off the set, out of the studio, and into the street, while the crew runs out after him, terrified. Meanwhile, I am left alone on the set with a nine-hundred-pound lion in my lap, purring contentedly.

But back to Larry. As I said before, to this day I love and respect Larry, both as an actor and as a human being. Nonetheless, I feel that, in the interests of television history and of accuracy, it's time to tell the whole, unvarnished truth about what really happened behind the scenes on *I Dream of Jeannie,* shocking as some of it is.

Larry himself has made no secret about the fact that he was taking drugs and drinking too much through many of the *I Dream of Jeannie* years and that he has regrets about how that impacted him. And I, of all people, know that I can't afford to be judgmental about the lure of drugs and the dreadful repercussions of taking them.

But this is one of my more startling memories of Larry while filming *I Dream of Jeannie.* Jeannie blink: Sally Field is filming *The Flying Nun* on the next sound stage, and one morning a group of elderly nuns pay a visit to the set. Afterward, someone comes up with the bright idea of bringing them over to the *I Dream of Jeannie* set for a visit as well.

So here they are, about ten of them: sweet, gentle, and demure in their black-and-white habits, their hands folded, their eyes bright with anticipation at the thought of visiting another Hollywood set and meeting all of us. Larry takes one look at the nuns, grabs an axe (which one of the technicians happens to have in the studio that day), and swings it around his head so ferociously that he could easily have killed someone. As he swings it, he lets out a torrent that includes every single foul swear word I've ever heard, and some I haven't—right in the stunned nuns' faces. If that isn't enough, he starts hacking at the cables frenetically until someone grabs the axe, frog-marches Larry off the set, then escorts the shaken nuns out of the building. It's hardly surprising that no visitors were ever allowed on the *I Dream of Jeannie* set again.

Sally and I were often in makeup at the same time. When I was rehearsing my Las Vegas nightclub act while I was working on *I Dream of Jeannie,* I used to arrive at the makeup department at six in the morning, with my little tape recorder with a tape of all my music in it, and learn my songs for my act while the makeup artist was applying my makeup.

Recently, in an interview, Sally let slip, "The only uncomfortable thing about doing *The Flying Nun* was, my God, Barbara Eden singing all the time in the makeup room at 6 AM and never stopping!"

Sorry, Sally! If only I'd known, I'd have practiced in the shower instead.

But back to Larry. After Sidney Sheldon suggested that Larry see a therapist and he agreed, the therapist was frequently on the set during filming of *I Dream of Jeannie,* in case he was needed. But even he didn't seem able to put the brakes on Larry. Consequently, Larry's dramatics escalated, and—now that we live in an X-rated age—could most likely become the basis of a terrific comedy series themselves.

In fact, you could devote a whole episode to the time when Sammy Davis Jr. guested in "The Greatest Entertainer in the World" and ended up threatening to kill Larry, and another to the time we filmed "The Second Greatest Con Artist in the World" in Hawaii with Milton Berle.

But there is one episode that I don't think would actually make it onto the air even today: the time when Larry, in frustration and anger at what he saw as the show's shortcomings and the second-string status of his character, Major Tony Nelson, relieved himself all over the *I Dream of Jeannie* set.

I'll be sharing more of Larry's tantrums in the rest of the book, no holds barred. But working with Larry was still a walk in the park in comparison to many other things that happened to me throughout the years, particularly in my private life—my stillborn son; two divorces; the death of Matthew, my only child, when he was thirty-five and on the threshold of marriage; and the loss of my beloved mother.

Through it all, my mother's voice has always echoed in my mind: *Rise above it, Barbara Jean, rise above it!* I've tried as hard as I can to do so. Sometimes I've triumphed and risen above whatever life has flung at me, but other times I've failed dismally, floundered, and been utterly swamped. This is the story of all those times, good and bad, better and worse, exactly how they happened, exactly how I coped, and exactly how I didn't.

chapter 1

A MAGICAL

CHILDHOOD

* * * * * * * * * * * * * * *

WHENEVER I HEAR the blare of a foghorn or see a picture of a mermaid or a young couple madly in love, I feel as if I've been Jeannie-blinked back into my childhood, happy and secure.

The foghorn, you see, reminds me of San Francisco, where I grew up. The mermaid reminds me of Dolfina, the famous "Girl in the Fishbowl" always on display at the Bal Tabarin restaurant in North Beach, where my parents often used to bring me when I was very young, simply because they couldn't afford a babysitter and had to cart me everywhere with them.

In those far-off years during the Depression, however poor my parents were, they still hadn't forgotten how to love, how to laugh, and how to dream. They were young and carefree, spent every penny my father earned from his job as a telephone lineman, and understood exactly how to have fun.

At the time, long before my younger sister, Alison, was born, I was my mother's "onliest only," as she called me then, and would until her dying day. Like many an only child, I was probably grown-up before my time, and those nights at the Bal Tabarin (which later became Bimbo's 365 Club), where Rita Hayworth danced in the chorus and Ann Miller was discovered dancing when she was just thirteen, only served to make me more mature and at the same time give me an early love of show business.

So did seeing Bob Hope perform live onstage when I was just four years old. My mother and father took me to his show at a local theater, and I remember how joyful watching Bob made me feel. Little did I know that when I grew up, I would meet him, we'd become friends, and I'd appear onstage with him many, many times myself.

When I was a small child, my dream was to be not an actress but a singer. Each night, when I did the dishes with my mother, Alice, she sang Gilbert and Sullivan ditties or tunes from her father's favorite Irish operetta, *Bohemian Girl,* and I joined in. I developed a passion for singing early on in my childhood, which was only further heightened when I sang in the church choir every Sunday.

At the same time, fishing on Fisherman's Wharf with my father (although the sight of fishermen gutting their fish put me off fish for life—to this day I never eat it), roller-skating along the wharf, and bicyling in Golden Gate Park with him all contributed to making me a bit of a tomboy (which, by the way, I always thought Jeannie was as well).

I've always considered myself a California girl and have been proud of it, but in reality I was born in Tuscon, Arizona. And I always relished looking back at my mother's family history and reconstructing exactly how I ended up being born there.

I still have a remarkable letter she gave to me, which was originally bequeathed to her by her mother. It was written in 1856 by my great-great-great-grandfather, John A. Bills, to my great-great-grandparents, Bilista and William Long, after they were forced to leave New York State and go west because William, a housepainter, was dying of lead poisoning. If I could have, I would have framed it, but it is too old and too fragile, so I keep it in an acid-free envelope.

All in all, I think it's a fascinating historical document (but if you don't, just skip it).

Ramsey, Illinois 28 Nov. 1856
Dear Daughter,
We rec'd your letter a few days ago and hasten to answer. We were sorry to hear that William was so feeble although it was not all together unexpected. He has been so long sick that we sometimes almost believed that thought he might at last recover—but we feel that even this letter may find you a widow and the children orphans—I sometimes feel as though you would be doubly afflicted situated as you are a stranger almost in a far off country—but it seem you are not discouraged or cast down entirely. We really hope a way will be provided for you and the little ones. Do you still feel that you had rather stay there or would you like to come back and live among your old acquaintances and friends once more.

We have sold out all our things in Troy and moved to the west. We are on a farm in a town called Ramsey it is on the Illinois South Central Railroad. As far south nearly as St. Louis. We have a very nice farm of 1110 acres and so far like it much. Gardner and George are here with us and John in Vandalia 13 miles south of us to work at his trade (dentist). Uncle Loren is out in the northern part of this state with all of his family and they seem and write that they like first rate. Uncle Alanson is still in New York. Alonzo has gone to sea again this time to Calcutta. I suppose he is bound to be a sailor. Iarne and Abner are in stores. Claryou is at home. Samuel and Sarah live in Williamsburg opposite New York. Daniel is a carman, Uncle Luis and Nathan are in (?) on their old places all well. Allen and Ester lived in Albany when we came away—have not heard from them since.

I had a letter from Mrs. Harlow sometime since they live in

*Oroville and she seems to think that they are getting rich again—
I hope they may. I suppose Mrs. Alfred Smith is out there as she has
sold all her furniture and was calculating to go in a few days when
we left Troy the first of July—is she there and what are they about.
I wish we could run in and see you and help you in your time of
need—but we are a great way apart and it is not likely that I shall
ever go to California again—if we had Mary & Willie home we
could give them a good chance for school and bread and milk—We
have two good cows and make plenty of butter and have lots of
cream and milk to eat and use—I suppose they are great children
now and hope they are and always will be good children and do all
they can to help their mother through life.*

*Now Bilista I should like to know how you are situated to
get a living—can you earn enough to make yourself and children
comfortable—do you intend to stay there and work and do all
you can to make a living or do you sometimes wish you was back
again—I wish you would write me as to how you feel about it—
We think this is a good and healthy country—My health and your
mother's is much better than it was in Troy and so far we are not
sorry we moved—Please write soon and often and we will write
often now that we are settled down once more—Give our respects to
Mr. & Mrs. Smith if she is there—and finally give our respects to
all our old acquaintances if you see any of them.*

*Goodbye and may the Lord give you strength to endure
whatever you may be called to go through.*

*Direct your letter "John A Bills, Ramsey-Fayette Co Illinois."
Your Father John A Bills*

*Mrs. Bilista A Long
San Francisco
Cal*

The Mary mentioned in the letter was my great-grandmother, Mary Dorothea Long, who came west in the covered wagon with her parents, Bilista and William Long, when she was only four years old. After her parents' untimely deaths, she was raised by nuns in San Francisco.

My great-grandfather, Richard O'Leary, was born in County Cork, Ireland. When he was a child during the potato famine, his parents, hoping to save his life, put him on a ship bound for the New World. That ship turned out to be one of the "coffin boats," so named because so many children who sailed on them died of starvation or disease during the harsh and unforgiving Atlantic crossing.

Richard O'Leary was one of the lucky ones; he survived. At fifteen years old, still unable to read and write, he took a job building the transcontinental railroad and ended up in Marysville, California, where he met a priest and confided to him that he wanted a wife.

The priest relayed that information to my great-grandmother, Mary, who thought about it for a bit, then informed the priest, "I'll walk out with him." So that's what she did, for just one week, at the end of which she announced to the priest, "I'll marry him," and did.

She went on to teach my great-grandfather to read and write, and had nine children along the way as well, one of whom was my maternal grandmother, Frances Elvira O'Leary, who was born in Nevada and went to school there.

Meanwhile, back east in Pennsylvania, my maternal grandfather-to-be, Charles Benjamin Franklin (a distant relative of the great man himself), the son of an Englishwoman, was orphaned at nine after his parents were killed in a carriage accident.

On discovering that young Charles had been left alone in the world, his two maternal aunts sailed from England to America, determined to bring him back home to the old country with them.

The aunts realized Charles was happy in his new home and allowed my grandfather to stay. However, later, he ran away from home, apprenticed himself to a ship's carpenter, and sailed the seven seas.

By the time Charles arrived back in America, he had married, divorced, and along the way become an accomplished carpenter, adept at all branches of the trade, including cabinetry. Finally he turned up in Nevada, where he booked into a small boardinghouse. There, one morning, a beautiful young girl—Frances Elvira O'Leary—served him breakfast.

Although he was entranced by her charms, he nevertheless couldn't help noticing that she kept rubbing her cheek. Without any preamble, he demanded to know why she hadn't seen a dentist. She blushed scarlet and shook her head, whereupon he grabbed her arm and declared, "Whether you like it or not, I'm taking you to one."

He did, and within months, my grandmother, Frances Elvira O'Leary, married Charles Benjamin Franklin in San Francisco. My mother, Alice, the youngest of four children, was born in El Paso. My grandfather became a house builder and would remain so for the rest of his days, building homes in Los Angeles, El Paso, and Tuscon, Arizona, which is where I came in.

During the first two or three years of my life, because money was quite scarce, we lived in Tucson and then El Paso with my grandparents. My earliest memory is of sleeping in one bed with my mother, in the morning watching her get dressed for work, and being overwhelmed by her youth and beauty.

In the early thirties, my mother attended business college, where she learned dictation and accounting, and eventually she got a job at the Western Auto Company. In many ways, she was ahead of her time, and truly emancipated. Thinking back to my pioneer great-grandmother and my schoolteacher grandmother,

I'd have to say that I was born of strong women, and that thought makes me proud.

Yet these women were also warm and loving, and I'll always remember how lucky I felt as a little girl to have my mother's hand to hold on to, and my grandmother's as well. My grandmother would hold my hand loosely, my mother more firmly, but either way, they both made me feel safe and loved.

My mother was the baby of her family and was particularly close to her sister, Margie, who lived in San Marino, not far from LA (of which more later). Margie was as pretty as my mother, possessed a vivid, whimsical imagination, and christened everyone in the family with secret fairy names. I was dubbed "Music." My mother was "Smile." And Aunt Margie called herself "Mischief."

I guess I must have inherited Aunt Margie's fanciful imagination, because from the time I was a small child, I had three fantasy friends: Dagolyn, a girl; Good Johnny, a boy; and Bad Johnny, who I believed lived under my bed. Dagolyn and the two Johnnies were always a rich and vibrant part of my childhood imagination, though I loved Good Johnny best. Looking back, I can't help wondering at the coincidence that my current husband, the love of my life, is named Jon.

Margie and my mother loved practical jokes and were always playing tricks on each other and the rest of the family. One time, my father (who didn't like anyone to look at his feet, and always made sure to wear slippers or shoes) was fast asleep, and Margie and my mother sneaked into his room. While he was snoring away, they pulled back the bedcovers and painted his toenails red. When he woke up and caught sight of his bright red toenails, he went ballistic, but then calmed down and laughed uproariously.

Another time, one of my uncles, who worked for the government, had to attend a crucial business meeting, and when he wasn't looking, Margie and my mother sewed up one of his pant legs so he couldn't get it on. They were always playing practical jokes like that, and I was always vastly entertained by all their pranks, however childish.

My grandfather, Charles Benjamin Franklin, was a loving and kind man who took great care of me. At the end of most days, he'd put his snap-brimmed hat on, say, "Get your hat, Barbara Jean" (which is what my grandparents and everyone else called me back then), take me by the hand, and set off for the grocery store with me.

On the way back, he'd always stop at a bar and have a beer; I had a soda. One day I came home and informed my grandmother that I'd drunk a whole glass of beer all by myself. Such was the force of the conviction in my voice that she believed me and practically had a fit until my grandfather convinced her otherwise.

My grandfather had beautiful reddish brown curly hair, and I remember when I was about three and asked, "Can I wash your hair, Grandpa?" and he let me. Even then, it was clear that he couldn't refuse me anything.

One day I begged him to buy me a pair of red shoes, and he did. When my grandmother saw them, she screamed, "Charles!" and whisked them away from me, putting them out on the fence. My grandfather and I exchanged rueful glances, but both of us knew better than to go against my grandmother's iron will. By morning they had vanished, and I never saw them again.

Another time, I overheard my mother and my grandmother saying that they were going to the movies. Off they went, leaving me at home with my grandfather. I went over to him, tugged on his coattail, and said, "Grandpa?" Without looking up from his newspaper, he said, "Yes, child?" Encouraged, I went on, "Grandpa, would you take me to the movies?" Without a moment's pause he said, "Yes, child." Then he put on his hat, and off we went together.

*

At the movies, we won a raffle, and brought home our prize, a case of Dr Pepper, so we couldn't hide our outing from my grandmother after all. Whether or not she minded, I'll never know. But the memory of my grandfather's good nature and abiding desire to please me always makes me happy.

My grandmother may have been puritanical and a little stern, but she also loved me without reservation. When I was about three, she and my mother became worried that I was thin and listless, so they took me to a doctor. The doctor took one look at my white, pinched little face and decreed, "She's a hothouse flower! She needs sun. Get her outside and let her play in the mud. She's far too clean."

So my grandmother took me into the garden, presented me with a spoon and a can, and showed me how to make a mud pie, while I squirmed in distaste. And even though I obeyed my grandmother's instructions to the last letter, as soon as I'd finished making one pie, I'd run inside the house and plead for her to wash my hands immediately.

I still remember vividly my grandparents' house on Upson Avenue in El Paso—where my red shoes disappeared. It was built in the Victorian style, with a little walkway going around the porch. About four years ago, I was booked to do a show in New Mexico, and flew into El Paso. A couple of sheriffs were on hand to drive me over the state line to the theater, and on the way I asked them to take me by my grandparents' house. It was still standing, and I was pleased.

When I was five, we moved to 1207 Bush Street in San Francisco. I attended my first school, Redding, and my life began in earnest. Not that I was happy to leave home for school. I felt far too safe and secure at home to want to venture out into the world, and I would much rather have stayed at home with my mother and my grandmother.

In fact, leaving my serene cocoon of home and family and being hurtled into school was a severe shock for me. On my first day there, my only happy moment was opening my lunch box and finding the sandwiches my mother had so painstakingly made for me that morning—a little piece of home.

I might have eventually settled down in school, but one day—just after I started the first grade—I looked up at the blackboard and suddenly couldn't see a single word written on it. My parents were petrified that I might be going blind, and although the doctor's diagnosis of a lazy eye was a relief, my mother still cried bitterly.

At the time, I couldn't grasp the reason, but when the very next day the doctor hooked a black patch onto my glasses ("We must cover the strong eye and make the lazy one work" was his edict) and ordered me to wear it all the time, I understood the reason for my mother's tears.

Funnily enough, none of the other children at school gave me a hard time about the patch. My only worry, though, was that I wouldn't be able to read properly. I loved reading so much, and still do. Learning to read had opened a whole new world up to me, and my mother always said that I went to school one day, and the very next began to read without stopping.

My mother and aunt got me my first library card when I was in the first grade, and I read *The Wizard of Oz* and all L. Frank Baum's other books, and *The Secret Garden*.

Although I spent hours and hours reading, lost in my imagination and quiet as a mouse, I still wasn't an easy child to raise. I always questioned everything. I'd usually end up doing what I was told, but not without running through a long list of questions first. In fact, I once overheard a relative clucking to another of the aunts, "Alice is going to have her hands full with that one!" I felt a flash of pride, but the reality is that I was never much of a rebel.

*

Part of the reason was that I loved my mother so much, but I also knew that rebelling wasn't polite and, more than anything else, I'd been schooled in politeness. Right through my childhood and way into my teens, whenever I went out, my mother always reminded me, "Always make sure you have your please, your thank you, and your handkerchief in your pocket."

After the attack on Pearl Harbor in 1941, I also had an innate sense that we were living in dangerous times and that my parents were struggling to survive; I feared I could lose them at any minute in a bombing raid. After the United States entered World War II, San Francisco was on high alert. There were air raid alerts practically every night, blackouts were mandatory, and even the lampposts were partly painted black. I remember having to go to school with a little dog tag around my neck, which bore my name and address and the name of the person to contact if I were lost or wounded during an air raid.

Meanwhile, my parents were doing their utmost to scratch out a living. My father worked very, very hard doing PBX wiring on ships, which kept him out of the army. Other than that, he worked at Pacific Bell Telephone his entire adult life, until he became seriously ill and couldn't work anymore.

His illness first manifested itself when he was traveling home from work on a streetcar and started vomiting blood. The doctors were puzzled to find cuts in his stomach; they speculated that ground glass somehow might have gotten into his food and that he unknowingly ate it, but none of the doctors ever knew for sure. Eventually he healed and went back to work, but he was never the same again. He became very angry and started to drink heavily. In the end, my parents had to sell their house on Forty-fifth Avenue so they could pay his medical bills. But although Mom and Dad were upbeat about the house sale, nothing was ever the same between them again.

*

In 1969 I was living in Sherman Oaks and married to my first husband, Michael Ansara, when I got a call from my mother telling me that my father had passed away from a cerebral hemorrhage, caused by a surge of high blood pressure. Afterward, paramedics found a great many blood pressure pills in his pocket. Though they had been prescribed for him, he had opted not to take them, for reasons I'll never know. I felt guilty that I hadn't been around to convince him to take the medication and that I hadn't gone to visit him more often. I still feel I haven't thanked him sufficiently for the man that he was. He worked so hard to support us.

My mother worked right through the war and after, as the credit manager for a Granat Brothers jewelry store. She didn't own much good jewelry herself except for a watch and her wedding ring, but even if she wore costume pieces, people routinely stopped her in the street and asked her where she'd gotten them. She had a wonderful, inborn sense of style that never left her, not even at the end of her life when she was frail.

My parents' financial existence was so perilous that we moved around a great deal. I attended five different schools in San Francisco, and we lived in five different homes, including one we shared with my aunt Margie and her husband.

We also spent a great deal of time with my great-aunts, Aunt Nora, Aunt May, and Aunt Nell, and with my great-uncles, Uncle Will and Uncle Tom, who lived in San Leandro and Vallejo, across the Bay. We'd go to visit them via the ferry, and when we'd come home very late at night, the foghorns would blare and I'd feel extremely sleepy and happy. I look back on those nights with warmth and affection.

Once I became a teenager, though, those happy times were punctuated by the occasional tussle with my mother over clothes, makeup, and of course boys. In high school I wasn't really attractive;

I was thin, underdeveloped, and geeky-looking. Even if I had wanted to improve my appearance, my mother would have stood in my way. She was very strict: she frowned on lipstick, and even if she had allowed me to wear more fashionable clothes, we simply couldn't have afforded them. Later on, she drilled into me that I shouldn't go steady too soon, and that I definitely shouldn't marry early in life. In retrospect, I believe she wanted me to remain a little girl for as long as possible.

I don't know whether it was due to the era in which I grew up or the way I was raised, but I was really sheltered, not in the least bit like teenagers today. I was so very square. I was banned from ever swearing; once, when I was long since an adult, my mother and I saw a swear word written on the sidewalk, and she went white and said, "Barbara Jean Huffman! That is *not* a good word."

Such was my mother's power over me that even when I appeared as the madam in a production of *The Best Little Whorehouse in Texas* and the script called for me to repeatedly utter a four-letter word (one beginning with the letter *f* and ending in *k*), I initially couldn't bring myself to say it.

I didn't know anything about the facts of life until I was thirteen or fourteen, when my mother, who secretly believed that she was extremely progressive, read me a few excerpts from a book, *Being Born.* I must have given her a blank look, because she proceeded to have a whispered conversation with my father.

"Harrison, you're her father. You have to tell her about it. She has to know," she said.

My father gave a weary sigh.

"You've got a part in this, Harrison, whether you like it or not."

"All right, Alice, all right," my father said. "At breakfast, I'll have my robe open and she'll see the hair on my chest."

So the very next morning, that's exactly what he did: left his robe open so the hair on his chest was visible to me.

I blushed and looked away.

He saw my reaction and stuttered, "Barbara Jean, I—I just want you to know that as you get older, there will be body changes, so don't be surprised or shocked by them."

He didn't say a word about the hair on his chest, and I remained none the wiser until a couple of girls at school set me straight and I finally learned what sex was all about.

* * * * * * *chapter 2* * * * * *

SHOW BUSINESS
BEGINNINGS

* * * * * * * * * * * * * *

EVEN WELL INTO my teens, dating wasn't much of a priority for me, and I wasn't at all bent on having any romantic entanglements, simply because my whole life revolved around my love of singing. From the time that I could first talk, I was determined to grow up and become a singer. Luckily for me, my mother—always my biggest cheerleader—supported me every step of the way.

Apart from singing with her while we did the dishes together (she washed, I dried), whenever we had company I used to entertain them with a song or two. One day when I was fifteen, my mother's best friend, Elinor Hoffman, slipped me a hundred-dollar bill (which was probably equivalent to a thousand dollars in today's money) and said, "Barbara Jean, you're genuinely talented. You should study singing and this ought to help you."

I was thrilled and, with my mother's approval, immediately enrolled in the San Francisco Conservatory, where Isaac Stern and Itzhak Perlman also studied (though not at the same time as me). There I had a fateful chance encounter.

One morning, Lorraine Hinton, a beautiful blond singing student who always wore extremely high heels (and later changed her name to Lori Hart) became ill and had to leave class early. Before she did, she begged me to cover for her in a gig that night.

Well, in those days, I didn't even know what a gig was, but Lorraine swiftly enlightened me. She explained that I'd have to put on my prettiest dress and sing a couple of songs with a dance band at the Garden Room in the Claremont Hotel, high atop a hill overlooking Berkeley, and afterward I'd be paid twelve dollars.

Whoopee! Twelve whole dollars for doing what I'd always dreamed of doing! So I rushed home and put on my pink taffeta gown (the one my parents had bought me for my first formal school dance), which had puffed sleeves and a sweetheart neckline. My mother lent me a tiny gold heart on a chain, and before I knew it, I was on my way to the Claremont Hotel.

A glamorous resort built on thirteen thousand acres by a rich Kansas farmer as a tribute to his wife and daughter, the Claremont Hotel was built in the style of an imposing English castle. It was the ideal setting to launch my cherished dream of becoming a singer.

My first song was "Blue Moon," and as I sang to an audience of tourists and businesspeople sipping cocktails, I made sure to lower my soprano voice in the hope that I would sound more grown-up, maybe even sexy.

From the stage, I could just make out my mother in the front row, because then—and always—my astigmatism meant that most of the faces in the audience were blurred. It was both a blessing and a curse, particularly when I was playing Las Vegas in later years and could never be entirely sure whether the crowd was focused on me or on their dinner, whether they were chatting or enjoying my act.

The flip side of my astigmatism, by the way, is that sometimes when I'm walking through a hotel lobby or boarding a plane and smile in the direction of a group of people, when I get closer to them I find out that they are total strangers. Consequently, more men than I'd care to remember have jumped to the conclusion that I'm trying to pick them up when I am not!

Anyway, that first night at the Claremont glided by like a beautiful dream, and I knew without a shadow of a doubt that I wanted to perform again as often as possible. Fortunately, in a community like San Francisco, word traveled fast, and soon I was receiving offers to sing at other venues. Next thing I knew, I was entertaining at the officers' club at Fort Ord and performing in USO shows, mostly at Camp Roberts, not far from San Francisco.

One memorable night, dressed to kill in an elegant peach satin gown, I walked out in front of an audience of fifteen thousand GIs, all hooting, wolf-whistling, and stamping their feet. Then the band struck up the first notes of the song I was supposed to sing: "Bewitched, Bothered and Bewildered."

All of a sudden, my mind went blank and I just couldn't remember the first line of the song. Even though I hadn't sung a word yet, the audience started throwing coins at me (I never figured out why). Through it all, I just kept smiling into what looked like a vast black pit. I felt like passing out, but no such luck.

So I leaned over to the bandleader and told him to start again and play "Blue Moon" instead. He did and rescued me, although that evening will always remain in my memory as one of the most embarrassing of my entire life.

But I'm jumping ahead. During my time at the Conservatory and then at City College, although I was living at home, I still wanted to earn a living, so I worked four hours a day in a local department store, selling and wrapping gifts. Later I got another job operating an IBM machine at the Wells Fargo bank, and in between I did my fair share of babysitting for friends and neighbors.

*

Consequently, during my teens, I was mostly all work and very little play because my primary focus in life was on performing and on my singing career.

My mother changed all that when one night after watching me rehearsing for the band, she looked at me thoughtfully and said, "Barbara Jean, you are hitting every note perfectly. The trouble is that the lyrics don't mean a thing to you. You aren't *feeling* a single word that you're singing."

After I recovered from my hurt feelings, I took a deep breath, conceded that she was right, and agreed to start acting lessons right away. By some quirk of fate, my mother had just finished listening to Carol Channing being interviewed on the radio and had heard Carol mention that she'd studied acting at Elizabeth Holloway's drama school, right there in San Francisco. When my mother told me about the interview, I enrolled for night classes there as well.

After a few weeks, Miss Holloway, a tiny woman who always had a colorful chiffon scarf draped around her neck, sent for me and, to my delight, offered me a scholarship to study acting full-time at her school.

I jumped at the opportunity, quit college, and started at Miss Holloway's immediately, studying not just acting but also fencing, tap dancing, and everything else I could about every aspect of show business.

One of Miss Holloway's most-repeated and invaluable pieces of advice was that all her students should attend as many auditions as possible, just for the experience. I followed her instructions to the letter but didn't get very far, until the day came when she called me into her office and told me that I ought to audition for the upcoming Miss San Francisco pageant.

Now, I'm not and never have been shy. Reserved, yes. Cautious, definitely. But shy, no. Still, the idea of parading up and down in front of a crowd of people who had assembled there for the sole purpose of judging not my acting or my intelligence but my face and my body filled me with dread.

But Miss Holloway brushed all my objections aside with a flick of one of her ubiquitous chiffon scarves.

"Whether you win the contest or not, you have to try, Barbara Jean," she said. "Go down and audition, and if they reject you, it doesn't really matter. At least you will have tried."

I nodded glumly.

But instead of being pleased and grateful that I was taking her advice, Miss Holloway had a parting shot for me.

"And Barbara Jean, you really do need to toughen up," she said.

My mother presumably agreed, because instead of recoiling in horror at the thought of me entering a beauty contest, she got to work and made me a sparkling royal blue strapless gown with a low waist and a hoop skirt, so that I'd look my best at the pageant.

I realize that nowadays thousands of young girls enter beauty pageants without batting a single false eyelash, but for me it was torture to parade up and down in my bathing suit while a panel of judges appraised me from head to toe. I felt as if I might as well have been naked. And I was unutterably shocked when I won the title of Miss San Francisco, along with a blue satin ball gown and a teeny-tiny diamond ring.

But my beauty pageant ordeal wasn't over yet. As Miss San Francisco, I was now obliged to enter the Miss California pageant. I didn't expect to win, and I didn't, but I liked the other girls, and we had a good time together. When the contest was over, I was flattered to be voted the friendliest and most cheerful girl in the pageant, the one with the best personality—a good egg. Other than that, I was relieved that my beauty pageant career was now well and truly over.

I guess, though, that Miss Holloway was right about one thing:

taking the plunge and appearing in the beauty pageant did give me confidence, although it didn't serve to toughen me up in the least. That would come later, if at all.

Again following Miss Holloway's advice to audition for everything, I auditioned for and got a part in *Spring Crazy*, a musical written by former Ziegfeld Follies dancer Mary Hay Barthelmess and her daughter. And although the show closed after just three performances, having appeared in it meant that I was able to get my Actors' Equity card, a necessity for a working performer.

As time went on, I realized that winning the Miss San Francisco title had also been a bit of luck for me because, as a result, I was interviewed on a couple of local talk shows, and on one of them I met a portly gentleman with a walrus mustache, the comedian Solly Hoffman. His stock in trade (or should I say shtick?) was record pantomime, which is miming to a record.

After the show, he came up with the idea that we should do an act together. Never one to turn down the chance of a job (except, as I'll tell you much later, under the most stringent of circumstances), I immediately agreed, and the act Hoffman and Huffman was born.

From then on, Solly and I entertained for Hadassah, the Shriners—you name it. The act always started with Solly miming to a song. He would introduce me as the *shaineh shiksa* (the beautiful gentile girl), and I'd do three songs. The act invariably ended with us doing a record pantomime to "Aba Daba Honeymoon," the song made so famous by Debbie Reynolds, another *shaineh shiksa*.

So that was my life during my late teens: singing with bands, clowning with Solly Hoffman, working in the bank, and studying acting. It was hardly surprising that I didn't have a minute in which to date anyone.

Well, all right, I'll 'fess up; I did manage a second or two. His name was Al Ansara, and when I said his last name, it lingered in my mouth like the taste of rich milk chocolate. Naturally, I had no idea how much the name Ansara would come to mean to me a few years down the line. Al was a student at San Francisco University, a workaholic like me who was putting himself through school by driving a truck part-time.

Each afternoon when I left Miss Holloway's, Al would be outside in the street, waiting for me, and he'd drive me to my job at the bank downtown. At the end of the day, we'd grab a soda together, then he'd drive me home to my parents' house, always keeping a polite distance from me during the ride.

Then the great day came when Al invited me to a dance, and I floated up onto cloud nine and stayed there. But it quickly became radiantly clear to me that I wasn't his kind of girl. Quite simply, I just wasn't fast enough for him. He offered me a rum and Coke, and all I wanted was the Coke. He kissed me on the mouth, but anything else was out of the question, and he knew it. It was hardly surprising that we parted company soon afterward.

I guess I ought to have been heartbroken, but I wasn't, because my heart was now firmly fixed on something else. Or rather, some-*where* else. And not just anywhere, but a place only four hundred miles from San Francisco, though it might as well have been in another world, on another planet: Hollywood, California.

I wish I could say that I was so passionate about following my dream that I simply packed my bags without any hesitation and went off whistling a happy tune, without giving the future a second thought, but that really isn't the truth. In fact, it took the inspiring Miss Holloway to shake me out of my San Francisco complacency, to tear me away from my safe little world of dance bands, banking, and drama school.

"It's time, Barbara," she announced (by this time I'd lost the Jean). "It's time for you to jump out of the nest."

Seeing my alarm, she went on, "You're much too comfortable at home. You've got too much talent. Don't stay in San Francisco. New York or LA is the place for you."

My head was spinning, but I knew she was right. Nonetheless, my options hung in the air, tantalizing me with their rich promise. Broadway or Hollywood? New York or LA? I flashed back to my pioneering ancestors, escaping from the East Coast and risking untold dangers in the West.

Should I take a stab at conquering Broadway, which Miss Holloway seemed to think was as important as conquering Hollywood?

Or should I play it safer and stay closer to home by opting for Los Angeles, and try my luck in movies instead?

I spent many a night tossing and turning, but still couldn't make up my mind. After I told of my dilemma to my singing teacher, Edna Fischer, she came up with a unique solution. She confided in me that she had once consulted a famous psychic named Emma Nelson Sims. According to Edna, Emma's predictions and her subsequent advice based on them had been uncannily accurate. Edna believed in Emma's powers completely.

Looking back, I am surprised at my own courage in visiting a psychic, something I'd never done before, but the very first moment I met Emma all my misgivings immediately evaporated because she looked exactly like one of my great-aunts. An elegant gray-haired lady in severely tailored clothes, Emma sat extremely close to me and stared deep into my eyes with the most piercing gaze I'd ever encountered. Then she spoke.

Word for word, this is exactly what she prophesied for me all those years ago: "There's no doubt about it at all, Barbara Jean. You must immediately move to Hollywood and win a part on television there."

In those days, television was a fledgling industry, an ugly stepsister to the rest of show business. I was offended that Emma had even mentioned it to me.

"But I don't want to do that. I want to sing!" I said indignantly.

Emma gave me a wise and knowing smile.

"Ah, Barbara," she said, "we all want what we want. And you *will* sing. But your future is in television."

I shook my head in disbelief.

"I want to act in movies," I said.

Emma smiled again.

"You *will* act in movies, Barbara," she said. "But your true future is in television. It is in television that you will make your greatest mark."

I did my utmost to hide my sharp disappointment from her, thanked her for her advice, and went home, my head spinning. Polite as always, I didn't question the rest of her prediction, but secretly I was surprised that such a famous psychic could get it so wrong.

Make my mark on TV, indeed! Ridiculous!

* * *

Nonetheless, I took Emma's advice and decided to go to Los Angeles and not New York. I still didn't wholeheartedly abandon myself to the adventure without giving it a great deal of thought and planning. That's my nature. So instead of plunging in at the deep end and booking myself a hotel room in the heart of downtown Hollywood, I played it safe and arranged to stay with my aunt Margie and uncle Grandville in San Marino, just sixteen miles away.

I intended to commute from San Marino to Hollywood each day, imagining that the journey would be quick and uncomplicated.

By rights it should have been, but after I had my first experience with the LA transit system, a seemingly interminable journey on a hot, crowded bus, I quickly concluded that unlike San Francisco, Los Angeles County just wasn't a bus-friendly place.

However, things began to look up considerably when through a mutual friend I managed to wangle an introduction to Solly Biano, head talent scout at the Warner Brothers studio.

I was highly excited and intensely aware that this could prove to be my big break, so on the morning of my interview with Solly I painstakingly ironed my best plaid skirt and my nicest beige blouse, polished my best patent leather shoes until they shone brilliantly, and, last of all, donned my whitest of white gloves.

Uncle Grandville drove me to Burbank, and though I was probably more nervous than I'd ever been in my life, I took comfort in the fact that he decided not to leave me at the studio but would wait outside in his car while I had my interview.

So when I walked through the gigantic iron gates at Warner Brothers and the security guard gave me a pass, then directed me to Solly Biano's office, I didn't completely feel as if I were Little Red Riding Hood about to place herself at the mercy of the big bad wolf.

I relaxed further after the casting director's affable assistant showed me into the office and introduced me to Solly, a handsome blond, blue-eyed man with a mustache. He was courteous and started by asking me about my drama training, my home, and my family.

Then, all of a sudden and to my everlasting shock, he pulled out a picture of his daughter, Lonnie, and said, "See, honey, that's what you need. Big tits!"

Tits! He said *tits* to me!

I must have turned as white as my gloves, but he wasn't finished with me yet. "You're a pretty girl from a nice home," he said, "and you come from a good family. Problem is, you're *too* nice."

I brightened a trifle, but then he went on. "But you're not pretty enough, and you're not tough enough, either. Go back to San Francisco and marry the boy next door as fast as you can."

Now, as young and naive as I was, I had already made it a firm rule not to cry in front of anyone, and I wasn't about to break my rule, not then, not ever. But by the time I got back to the car and told Uncle Grandville what had happened, I found it difficult to hold back the tears.

My uncle, in contrast, wanted to go up to Solly Biano's office and give him what for. I spent the next ten minutes convincing him not to, by which time my tears had stopped and I had composed myself sufficiently for the drive home.

But once I got upstairs to the privacy of my room, I let go completely and sobbed till I felt like my head was about to explode.

Fifteen minutes later, I finally calmed down, and gave myself a stern talking-to. *Barbara Huffman, just you remember that Hollywood isn't only about mammary glands. You can act, so become a character actress.*

Then I dried my tears and promised myself I'd do just that. I also made up my mind to part ways with the Los Angeles County bus system as well.

Always cautious with money, I'd managed to save an impressive thousand dollars from all my band appearances and Hoffman and Huffman shows, so I bought a beat-up old Buick. My boyfriend, trumpeter Al Sunseri (who had worked with me in San Francisco bands), reupholstered and cleaned it until it shone like a newly faceted high-quality stone, and drove it down to LA for me.

My next step—and I suppose you could call it a leap, not a step—was to move out of my aunt and uncle's home and into the fabled Hollywood Studio Club, dubbed by cynics the "Hollywood Nunnery."

A little background here: Formed in 1916 by a group of aspiring actresses so they could read plays together, the Hollywood Studio Club first met in the Hollywood Public Library. However, in 1925, with the backing of Mary Pickford and Mrs. Cecil B. DeMille, as well as donations from Gloria Swanson, Douglas Fairbanks, Harold Lloyd, and Howard Hughes (you'll hear more about him later), the Studio Club later moved into a three-story Spanish-style steel-and-concrete building on Lodi Place, not far from Sunset and Vine, that was filled to the brim with antiques and overstuffed furniture.

From then on, the Studio Club, which was run by the YWCA, became sought after as a home for young Hollywood women who were involved in all aspects of show business. Provided that they could supply bona fide references, actresses, script girls, makeup artists, casting directors, secretaries, and anyone else in the business could live in the Studio Club, where they were easily able to pool information about auditions, rehearse, study, and in general network in order to further their burgeoning careers.

On my first day at the Studio Club, as fate would have it, I encountered one of the most famous Studio Club residents of all: Kim Novak, who'd lived there for the past five years but was moving out that very day. A silvery blond vision clad from head to foot in lilac, Kim had a handsome man trailing in her wake. I thought then that she was the most beautiful woman I'd ever seen in my life.

And there I was, grubby, sweat-stained, and worn out from moving box after box containing most of my worldly possessions—plaid dresses, patent leather shoes, white gloves, my best blue leather jewelry box (which would have pride of place in my room, although I didn't have anything in it except my tiny Miss San Francisco diamond ring), plus literally scores of books—into the Studio Club.

The dramatic contrast between Kim and me didn't make my

first day at the Studio Club any easier. Quite the reverse. And by the time I had moved everything into my room, I couldn't have felt more lost and lonely. A few weeks later I gained a roommate, a beautiful brunette actress named Barbara Wilson, who was a lot of fun.

My only pleasure came at the very end of the night when I called my aunt Margie and my uncle Grandville because I missed them so much. That call became a daily ritual because I couldn't afford to call my parents long-distance in San Francisco.

Years later, at the height of *I Dream of Jeannie*'s success, Aunt Margie let slip that she hadn't ever approved of my going into acting, because she didn't think the business would be good for me. I guess that my many evening calls from the Studio Club, in which I must have sounded extremely depressed, only served to reinforce her feelings. Nonetheless, she was encouraging and supportive, and stayed that way until she died in her nineties. I still miss her today.

Residence at the Studio Club included the use of the library, the laundry room, the sewing room, and the sundeck. In the midst of everything was the crucial notice board, where agents, producers, and directors posted news of upcoming auditions, and aspiring actors and actresses advertised for girls to read with them at auditions.

In my day, over a hundred girls lived at the Studio Club. Each of us paid fourteen dollars a week for a room, a telephone answering service, a cleaner twice a week, and two meals a day (generally breakfast and dinner, because no one had time for lunch), at which we all ate home-style food served on a buffet in a large dining room where we could all meet and gossip.

The only memorable thing about the Studio Club mealtimes is that one day when I was eating dinner in the dining room, all of a sudden—and I never discovered why he was there—John Wayne swaggered across the room, larger than life.

The only other celebrity I remember seeing at the Studio Club, apart from John Wayne and Kim Novak, was Mary Pickford, her hair arranged in big blond ringlets, rather like the style she wore in *Rebecca of Sunnybrook Farm,* even though she was now well into her sixties.

Ayn Rand, author of *The Fountainhead,* was one of the Studio Club's earliest residents. Like many of us, she was so poor that she couldn't afford to pay her rent, so a charitable benefactor donated fifty dollars. But instead of using the donation to pay her rent, Ayn promptly went out and splurged on a set of black lingerie.

Marilyn Monroe was another Studio Club resident who had trouble coming up with the rent. She finally raised it by posing for that notorious nude calendar, in which she reclined on red velvet. It caused a scandal, but made her an overnight star.

Marilyn was probably the biggest star ever to launch her career while living at the Studio Club, but other names aren't chopped liver, either: Dorothy Malone, who won an Oscar for *Written on the Wind* and who, during her time at the Studio Club, dated Mel Tormé; Diana Dill, who met and married Kirk Douglas while she was still living at the Studio Club; Donna Reed; Evelyn Keyes; Rita Moreno, of *West Side Story* fame; Sally Struthers; and tragic Sharon Tate, who was murdered by the Manson family.

Long before any of us had made it in the business, we knew that we had to abide by the club's stringent rules. For example, if we wanted to have a guest at the club for dinner, we were obliged to alert the staff a few days in advance, and get permission. Men of any age, of course, were not allowed to set foot in any of our rooms, which we had to keep spotlessly clean and tidy at all times.

The Studio Club was arranged around a courtyard, and the center of operations was the reception desk, right by the entrance, where Florence Williams, an attractive and imposing dark-haired woman, managed the club and ran a tight ship. She answered all our calls, took messages, and made sure to lock the Studio Club's doors at midnight sharp. We all knew that we had to be in at midnight without fail, or we would be locked out, no matter what. However, permission would be granted if we did request a pass to go away from the Studio Club for the night or the weekend, although we had to leave Florence a number and an address where, if necessary, we could be contacted.

The Studio Club's strict rules didn't trouble me much, as I wasn't planning to invite men into my room or be out late at night. In fact, because I wanted to be free to audition during the day but needed a salary in order to survive, I got a job in a local bank, which began at four and went on into the evening.

Otherwise, whenever I came back home to the Studio Club, I spent most of my time hanging around the notice board, answering as many of the advertisements as possible and auditioning for every single job around.

I was determined to make it in Hollywood, and I knew that auditioning for everything going—amateur as well as professional—was the only way in which I could become a successful actress, or at least survive financially.

At least that's what I believed. However, after about a month at the club, I was to discover that there might be an alternative route to survival in Tinseltown, one of which my aunt Margie definitely would have disapproved. And, to tell the truth, so did I.

chapter 3

A BABE IN

HOLLYWOODLAND

* * * * * * * * * * * * * *

IT WAS ONE of those smoggy Los Angeles mornings. I'd just come back from an audition for a car commercial that I knew I wouldn't get, and I was feeling rather despondent. As I trudged up the sweeping Studio Club staircase, Jolene Brand, a statuesque brunette actress who I knew was moonlighting as a showgirl at Ciro's nightclub on Sunset Boulevard, was coming down the stairs toward me.

She stopped and asked me to have coffee with her. I was due at the bank in two hours' time but was free until then, so I said yes.

Still a bit downhearted at not getting the commercial, I sat back and let Jolene do the talking. And, boy, did she talk! What was I doing at the Studio Club? What was my acting experience? And why was I working in a *bank*?

Ten minutes later, she got to the point. Why didn't I audition for the dance line at Ciro's, where she worked and which her boyfriend, George, managed?

"Because I'm afraid I can't dance," I explained patiently.

"Doesn't matter," Jolene declared. "Neither can I. Just come and audition, and I promise you, they'll love you."

"But I'm not like you, Jolene," I said.

"You don't have to be, Barbara. You're you, and that's quite enough," she said.

"But Jolene, you're tall! You've got very long legs. I'm not and I don't," I said, as if I were spelling out the facts of life to an Eskimo who couldn't speak a word of English.

"Just wear high heels and shorts, so your legs will look long and lean, and you'll be fine," Jolene said.

I was running out of excuses. And after all, I *had* done some tap and a little modern dance at Miss Holloway's. Besides, Jolene said that the club paid really well, and I was no stranger to nightclubs, having practically been raised at the Bal Tabarin. Little did I know that Ciro's was quite another ball game: the biggest, glitziest, most decadent nightclub in the whole country.

In those long-ago days of cafe society, customers dressed to the hilt before a night on the town, champagne and caviar flowed nonstop, and Marlon Brando, Frank Sinatra, Cary Grant, and Kirk Douglas routinely patronized Ciro's, bringing with them glamorous starlets galore, all willing and eager to cater to their every whim.

At that time, Ciro's was still at the height of its glory days: Peggy Lee, Sophie Tucker, Billy Eckstine, Nat King Cole, Dean Martin, and Jerry Lewis all performed at Ciro's, and Lana Turner, Judy Garland, and Marilyn Monroe were romanced there by glamorous men set on sweeping them off their feet. It was dinner at eight, a ten o'clock show, and afterward a night of unbridled passion. All in all, Ciro's vibrated with glamour and mystique, laced with an aura of sin and sensuality.

Ciro's catered to male customers unashamedly, and in the most artful ways. As I learned years later, no tall maitre d' was ever hired at Ciro's because the powers behind the club firmly believed that any short male guest would loathe following a tall maitre d' to his table.

Nor did Ciro's hang any mirrors in the main room, a strategy

*

to prevent revelers from catching a glimpse of how extremely debauched they looked as the evening wore on. Light fixtures were set on special dimmers all over the club, so that as the hours went by, the light faded slowly until the club closed at two in the morning.

I was unaware of that Ciro's lore then. All I cared about was that I had to learn four numbers for the audition and that hell would probably freeze over before I was transformed into the showgirl type. I was scared half to death.

But thanks to Miss Holloway's advice, I was going to try. So off I went, my heart in my mouth, to Ciro's on Sunset, where a Copa-style line of ten chorus girls danced fourteen ensemble numbers a night and, along the way, added to Ciro's erotic allure.

At the audition, my worst fears that I'd be truly humiliated by my own shortcomings were immediately confirmed when the choreographer positioned a group of Ciro's dancers in the front row and asked me to stand right next to them. The pianist thumped out a tune, I did a high kick, and my shoe flew right off my foot, up in the air, and down onto the stage again with a clunk.

I could have died, but the choreographer just motioned to me to pick it up and carry right on dancing, so I did. But as much as I struggled to follow the other girls' footwork, I couldn't keep up with the intricate dance steps and felt like a klutz of the first order. Then the music stopped, and the choreographer asked ten of us to come back to the club the following day. I nearly fainted when I found out I was one of them.

But I needed the job, so, like it or not, I went back to Ciro's again. At the second audition I realized that I wasn't the only klutz on the block. After watching many of us galumph around the stage like elephants, it began to dawn on me that Jolene had been absolutely right. Ciro's wasn't about excellence in dance. It was about something else altogether: pretty girls.

*

However, that realization didn't stop me from worrying about my own lack of dance ability. It was only years later that George Schlatter, who managed the club and later went on to produce *Rowan and Martin's Laugh-In* (and married Jolene along the way), cracked that I must have been nuts to worry about my footwork at the audition or while performing in the show. "We hired you because we knew the customers would never look at your feet, darling, but much further up," he said.

I was young and naive and just didn't fully understand the real reason male customers flocked to Ciro's in droves. But at least I wasn't lying about my age, like some of the other girls. A number of them, I later discovered, were much too young to be working there.

To my everlasting surprise, after the second audition I got the job, and what I look back on as my month in purgatory began. During my first few days at Ciro's, we rehearsed every afternoon, and I spent most of the time stumbling around, losing my shoes, treading on the other girls' feet, and, as soon as a break was called, bolting into the ladies' room, where I sobbed my heart out.

Then at four I'd rush over to the bank and start working there. After the bank closed, I'd speed back to Ciro's again, just in time for the ten o'clock show, where, to my horror, I was put in the front row of the chorus, presumably because I was so much shorter than all the other girls.

After a week, it was obvious to me that working at Ciro's and at the bank just didn't mix. Since I was making so much more money at Ciro's, I quit the bank and concentrated on my job in the chorus at Ciro's instead.

Fortunately, a dance team called the White Sisters took pity on me and spent some time teaching me the dance routines. I followed their instructions as best I could, but although I ended up not being such a klutz anymore, I still didn't feel comfortable working at the club. From my perspective, dancing at Ciro's felt like being on another planet. To top it all off, most of the girls mixed with the customers between shows—it wasn't mandatory, and I did not, but it happened a great deal.

Then George discovered that I could sing, so I was given the additional job of singing with Bobby Ramos and his band in between shows. The first show started at ten, the second at midnight, and each of them lasted an hour.

A short time later, I was given a number of my very own to perform in the show: Miss Adelaide's song "Take Back Your Mink," from *Guys and Dolls*.

Suddenly the other girls were at my throat like a herd of long-legged hyenas scenting fresh blood. Before, my failure to mingle with the male customers between shows had passed without comment. Now the girls—most of whom had the longest legs not in captivity and the sharpest nails in existence—turned on me with a vengeance, sniggering, "Here comes the Little Virgin."

They probably didn't like me any better after one of the girls was asked by Sammy Davis Jr. to give me a message. A big scowl disfigured her pretty face as she whispered to me, "Sammy would like to take you out." He was at the height of his career then, a big star (though his Rat Pack days were yet ahead of him), but I still wasn't about to go out with one of the customers.

Besides, I'd heard all about Sammy's wild parties, which he threw at his house high in the Hollywood Hills. George later confided to me that as soon as Sammy first saw the house (which once belonged to Judy Garland, and which had just been put on the market by the new owners) he fell in love with it and wanted to buy it then and there. But he was realistic enough to know that the current owner would never sell to someone of the Negro race (as African Americans were then called). So George stepped in and bought the house for Sammy, then transferred ownership over to him.

Anyway, I'd heard all about the girls who went to those parties, and sometimes ended up staying there. So I politely refused Sammy's invitation, and resorted to the white lie that I had a boyfriend, which at the time I didn't.

My innocence really ought to have been a protection in the jungle that was Ciro's, but it was not. It was more like a red rag to a bunch of heifers. When the girls found out that I regularly went to church, they mocked me endlessly. And later on I discovered that the male staff was secretly taking bets on who could first deflower the Little Virgin.

One night, George, who always kidded around with me, but in the nicest way, came over and told me that Elvis Presley had called him and asked if he could take me out on a date. I assumed George was kidding and told him so. I thought no more of it until just recently, when George and I were reminiscing about old times together and he told me that Elvis had indeed called him and asked him to arrange a date with me. Fascinating, in light of what happened between Elvis and me many years after I worked at Ciro's.

Fortunately, though, the other girls never found out that Elvis wanted to take me out. If they had, I'd have been toast. I was in way over my head at Ciro's and I knew it. I was surrounded by a bunch of tough, if beautiful, girls who all obviously despised me. Their venom reached such a crescendo that one day, just before the show, when we were lined up to use the bathroom (a little wooden cubicle, which for some unknown reason had a lock on both the inside and the outside) in our dressing room, they all ganged up on me.

When I entered the toilet enclosure, I suddenly heard a click. Hoping against hope that they hadn't done what I feared they'd done, I tried the door handle. Sure enough, it didn't open. Livid, I banged on the door, yelling, "Let me out! Let me out!"

There were hushed whispers outside the door, a few giggles, then the sound of footsteps receding. I banged on the door again. Then I heard the orchestra strike up the opening bars of my song. I dissolved into tears.

After a few minutes I heard the key turn in the lock, and the stage manager flung open the door. I fell into his arms, sobbing with a combination of relief and anger. Onstage, the number following mine was already in full swing. The girls had achieved their goal; I didn't sing "Take Back Your Mink" at Ciro's that night.

If I hadn't needed my salary so much, I probably would have thrown in the towel that night and never gone back to Ciro's again. But quitting was never my style, and I needed the job, so I gritted my teeth, and forced myself to go back to Ciro's the very next night. I went through my routines like a sleepwalker and ignored the other girls whenever possible. Which was probably just as well, because afterward, through the grapevine, I learned that they had all been severely reprimanded for what they had done to me, and for their malice and lack of professionalism. And while George later went on to dismiss the girls' cruelty to me as a sort of initiation or test they regularly gave to new Ciro's recruits, I just didn't see it that way at the time, and it hurt my feelings immeasurably.

A week later I was vastly relieved when, in the gentlest terms possible (some yarn centering around a dancer who needed the job so she could support her baby), George fired me. I almost cried with joy.

Looking back, though, I think Ciro's and Jolene did me a favor, because working there got me out of the rut of slaving away in a bank and propelled me into my new existence as a full-time, if struggling, actress.

*

At this point—particularly after my abortive stint at Ciro's and perhaps because, living in the Studio Club, the spirit of Marilyn may well have started to influence my choices—I jettisoned my plaid pinafores and went on a shopping spree at Jax in Beverly Hills, where I bought a sexy pink gingham dress with spaghetti straps and a scoop neck, as well as a pair of tight-fitting yellow pants, which probably accentuated what George Schlatter had kiddingly termed my "bubble butt."

Then I saw a Studio Club ad for a young actress to read with an actor auditioning at Warner Brothers. Remembering the Warner Brothers talent scout Solly Biano and how he had rejected me, I shivered at the words "Warner Brothers." But I squared my shoulders and answered the ad, and before I knew it, I was walking through the studio gates once more. Only this time Uncle Grandville wasn't waiting outside in his car to console me if I failed.

At first, the memory of the casting director made me feel nauseous, but I quickly recovered and did the scene with the actor. Afterward, the studio's acting coach, Don Cutler, offered me the chance to study with him on a daily basis, free of charge.

I was thrilled. I still hadn't been cast in a movie or a play, and very much wanted to improve my acting technique.

I took Don Cutler's class at Warner's every morning. One day I was walking toward the classroom when I heard a male voice behind me shout, "Hey, you!"

I didn't turn around. I just kept on walking.

"Hey, you! You in the yellow pants!"

I wanted to run, but my ingrained sense of politeness triumphed over my fear. I turned around to face Solly Biano, the man who had told me to go back to San Francisco.

I almost fainted dead on the spot. I didn't belong at Warner's. He was sure to have me thrown off the lot.

*

He gave me a big smile.

"Are you an actress?" he said.

I nodded mutely.

"Has the studio tested you?" he said.

I shook my head, incredulous. He didn't recognize me! Okay, I wasn't wearing white gloves or plaid anymore, but I was still the same girl he had rejected out of hand just five months earlier.

"Then we're going to test you right away," he said, and threw me another brilliant smile.

So the man who'd rejected me in the first place, the man who'd temporarily broken my spirit but then put iron in my soul, actually arranged for me to have a screen test at Warner Brothers after all.

And although I didn't get a contract at the studio, I'd learned a valuable lesson: no matter who rejects you in life, no matter how bad you feel, no matter how much that rejection hurts you, just keep on going. Put one foot in front of the other and ignore people's negative judgments, because those can change or even be forgotten.

So I carried on auditioning and didn't let the continual rejection get me down, until one day my persistence finally paid off.

I was over at Universal, doing another reading with yet another aspiring actor, when I met an agent, Wilt Melnick, a friendly man in his thirties with sandy hair and an engaging smile, who offered to represent me.

"But there is just one condition," he said.

My heart sank. By now I had wised up to Hollywood men and their "conditions," and I wasn't giving in to any of them. I raised an eyebrow and waited for the inevitable.

"The name Barbara Huffman sounds like a doctor," Wilt went on. "Change your name and I'll represent you."

In retrospect, I wonder whether a certain *Desperate House-wives* actress named Felicity was ever faced with a similar dilemma.

However, having met her at the 2006 Academy Awards (when she was nominated for *Transamerica*) and chatted about my former last name and her current one as well as our distant Huffman relatives, I know that she never once bowed to any hotshot Hollywood agent who demanded that she jettison her last name. Perhaps she was made of sterner stuff than I was, or perhaps times have simply changed.

In 1955, though, when Wilt Melnick issued his ultimatum that I change my name, I only hesitated for a few moments before replying.

"Mr. Melnick," I said, "just as long as I can carry on being called Barbara, you can give me any last name you like."

He gave me a long, appraising look.

"You seem kinda innocent," he said. "So let's call you Eden, like the garden."

That's how Barbara Eden was born.

By coincidence, Wilt Melnick also represented Kim Novak, though our paths never crossed again. However, early in my relationship with Wilt, I had a narrow escape from someone else also associated with the Studio Club—Howard Hughes.

Wilt called me there early one morning to tell me that I should expect a midnight call from Howard Hughes.

A warning light flashed in my head, but I trusted Wilt, so I kept silent.

"He'll ask you to come straight over to Republic Pictures to meet him, but don't be worried. He's really on the up-and-up. He's just an eccentric. Midnight is when he always interviews actresses. Those are his legitimate office hours and you'll have no problems with him," he said.

I wasn't reassured and made a deal with my roommate, Barbara

Wilson, that if Howard Hughes called, she'd chaperone me at the midnight meeting.

Fortunately, Howard Hughes never did call me, but I still can't help wondering what was going on in Wilt's mind when he suggested that I go over to Howard Hughes's place at midnight. I'd like to think that he was just looking out for me professionally. And I want to give him the benefit of the doubt, but perhaps I was—and still am—more than a little naive.

After all, Wilt was a top Hollywood agent and, unlike me, had no illusions about the town or the industry. In fact, how he got me my first job is just one example of the way in which the business worked back then, and the way in which the men who ran it viewed women—and probably still do.

"They want a sexy blonde over at CBS. So wear the gingham dress," Wilt instructed me.

The gingham dress? It was March and unseasonably cold, but I wasn't about to argue with Wilt. I threw on the dress, flung a woolly white coat over it, and drove right over to CBS.

The lobby was colder than a Sub-Zero refrigerator. In a moment of rebellion, I went up to the interview but didn't take my coat off.

The next morning Wilt called, irate. "Barbara, you didn't get it. Tell me you wore the dress. Tell me you wore it!"

Well, I could never bring myself to lie to Wilt.

"I wore the dress, Wilt, but I didn't take the coat off," I said.

To do him justice, he didn't give me a hard time.

Instead, he got me a second interview for the same job, but he didn't mince his words when he prepared me for it, either.

"For God's sake, Barbara, wear that tight gingham dress, and this time take that goddamn coat off!" he said.

Grateful to get another chance at the job, I wore the dress, and even before I arrived at the building I took my coat off. At the same time, I consoled myself that at least that way, I knew that I wouldn't have to peel off my coat at the audition like some kind of a stripper.

The director was urbane, kind, and polite. He asked me where I'd studied, then after a minute or two thanked me and I was dismissed. Gingham dress or not, I hadn't gotten the job.

But just as I was walking down the hall, a man lolling by the watercooler chatting with a group of other men detached himself, came over to me, and asked what I was doing in the building.

I explained I was there for an interview but that I clearly hadn't gotten the job. The man seemed sympathetic and asked me who my agent was, and that, I thought, was that.

When I got back to the Studio Club, there was a message to call Wilt.

"Bar, you got it!" he said, jubilant.

Mr. Watercooler, it turned out, was Nat Perrin, the producer of the show for which I'd just auditioned.

My very first job. Twelve spots on twelve live shows as a dumb blonde who sang off-key and appeared in skits with the star of the show, a new performer named Johnny Carson.

Later, I found out that the reason why the director hadn't immediately cast me in the show was because, as he later explained to me, apologetically, "When I found out where you had studied and for how long, I assumed that an intelligent girl like you could never pass for a brassy blonde who sings off-key. I'm afraid I jumped to the wrong conclusion."

Nat Perrin had set him straight, so now I had my first job, on *The Johnny Carson Show,* a live summer replacement for Red Skelton's show that was projected to run over the summer of 1955. Johnny was only twenty-nine at the time, married to his first wife,

Jody, but restless, insecure, and, I discovered afterward, drinking too much, perhaps to assuage his nerves at getting his big break at last.

Those nerves were never on display during the show, though. Johnny was brilliant at what he did, and really clever, but I could tell that the only time when he was really comfortable was when he was onstage. In private, he was quiet and extremely self-conscious.

No one could get close to Johnny even at that early stage in his career, least of all me—mainly because CBS gossip had it that, married or not, offstage Johnny had a taste for curvy blondes. As a result, whenever I was around Johnny, I wore armor, metaphorically speaking, and he probably sensed my reserve.

Perhaps I overreacted, because in fact Johnny always behaved like a perfect gentleman. As it happens, he lost his cool in my presence only once. A hapless secretary, unaware that Johnny was allergic to cats, brought hers to the studio, and Johnny visibly bristled when he saw it. The secretary was ordered off the set, and the show went on without any further incident, but I could tell that Johnny was upset.

Offstage Johnny was acutely sensitive, but onstage, like most comedians, he protected himself with a hard shell that might as well have been made of stainless steel and Teflon. That shell was impervious to any hurts, any slights, any rejections, and Johnny, like countless other comedians, wore it like a second skin and always would.

Decades later, I made six guest appearances on *The Tonight Show*. Johnny was nice to me, if impersonal. One time, at the end of the show, he threw in a brief mention that we'd worked together early in his career. I could tell that the memory of the days when he wasn't a big star deeply embarrassed him, and he didn't mention it again, either in public or in private.

*

However, when we both had Las Vegas acts but were appearing in different hotels, Johnny called out of the blue and invited me to spend the afternoon with him in his suite at Caesar's, complete with his own private rooftop swimming pool. I considered Johnny's invitation to be a friendly one, not romantic, and because I felt isolated and lonely in Las Vegas, I might have accepted. But my experience with the arid Las Vegas air was that if I went out in it for longer than a few minutes, I'd lose my voice entirely. I had two shows to do that night, so I couldn't afford to risk it. I sent word to Johnny, couched in the most courteous of terms, that I couldn't make it to his hotel. He was miffed, and from that moment on, whenever we met at parties or at other Hollywood events, his behavior toward me was cold, distant, and forbidding.

My early appearances on Johnny's show didn't exactly catapult me to stardom, but they did help advance my career slightly. A short while later, I was chosen by a group of Los Angeles press agents to be one of fifteen "Baby Wampus Stars"—supposedly up-and-coming starlets.

I enjoyed meeting the other girls, who included Jill St. John, Angie Dickinson, and Barbara Marx, who later married Frank Sinatra. A group of us were photographed for *Life* magazine at Harold Lloyd's glamorous estate, which boasted a beautifully decorated and gigantic Christmas tree that he left up year-round.

When I still failed to get any acting jobs, I posed for some pinup shots. There was never any question of my posing for anything salacious, although I did don a bathing suit for a photo session with the notorious Russ Meyer.

Around that time, I was photographed in a bikini for the cover of *Parade*, the Sunday newspaper magazine. I considered that I looked fairly demure in the photographs. Unfortunately, my great-aunts Nora and Nell vehemently disagreed, and they called to issue a sharp reprimand. How could I display my body to the world in such a wanton way?

As gently and kindly as possible, I explained that it was really a very modest swimsuit.

However, they refused to be pacified until my grandmother stepped in and calmed them down a bit. But the fact remained that until they died, Great-Aunt Nell and Great-Aunt Nora never approved of my modeling.

In many ways, though, they were on target. Modeling wasn't really for me, and I basically disliked doing it. So I was thrilled when Wilt called with the good news that I'd been cast in a small part on *The Ann Sothern Show,* a popular TV series.

My first on-screen appearance! I pored over the script excitedly and discovered that I was to play a fur-clad agent and deliver just three or four lines. I flashed back to Emma's prediction and smiled to myself. Make my mark on TV? Not with just three or four lines, I wouldn't.

If I had indeed harbored any delusions of grandeur regarding my appearance on the show, they would have quickly evaporated when—just as I had finished in makeup—Miss Sothern (given what happened next, I can't conceive of referring to her as Ann) stalked onto the set, a maid dressed in a classic black-and-white uniform in attendance. Then Miss Sothern swept right over to me, looked me up and down, turned around, and stalked away again. No response to my tentative hello. No smile, nothing.

I stood frozen to the spot, not knowing what to do next. Then the makeup man beckoned me to come back to makeup again because, he said, he needed to fix my face.

I sat quietly, bewildered and not quite understanding what was going on, while he redid my makeup.

The truth became agonizingly obvious when I heard him

whisper into the phone, "I'm sorry, Miss Sothern; there's nothing I can do to make her look bad."

Before I could get over my shock at the implications of what he'd said, I was called back on the set again.

There Miss Sothern fixed me with a look so glacial that it could have frozen Vesuvius.

"We don't need a rehearsal. Let's just shoot this and get it over with," she snarled in my direction.

For my first job in front of the camera, I said my lines as best as I could, then left, shaken to the core by my encounter with Miss Ann Sothern.

A witch on wheels, if ever there was one.

*   *   *

Fortunately, my next TV job, on a pilot, *The Jan Sterling Show,* proved to be a far pleasanter experience. Jan, an award-winning film actress, couldn't have been nicer (and off camera she had a great line about her husband and son: "Mummy works for toys, Daddy works for bread and butter"), so my faith in Hollywood divas was restored. Not that I was just working in Hollywood. I did a play, *Voice of the Turtle,* at the Laguna Playhouse with James Drury, which was notable in that I was spotted in it by a Twentieth Century Fox director, Mark Robson, who was soon to play a big role in my career.

Meanwhile, Wilt managed to get me a bit part in my first movie, as a college girl in *Back from Eternity.* I was grateful to get a job acting in a movie at last, and relieved that my Studio Club roommate, Barbara Wilson, was cast in the movie as well.

On the first day at the studio, I found it extremely weird to be working with producer-director John Farrow (Mia's father), who carried a cane everywhere with him. Perplexed, Barbara and I managed to waylay another extra and in a whisper asked her about it.

She gave a wry smile and said, "Just stay away from him if you can, because he loves to goose us girls with it!"

We took her advice.

Next, I got an even smaller part in an episode of the TV show *The West Point Story*, and then played a secretary in the movie *Will Success Spoil Rock Hunter?*

One of the highlights for me during that time was meeting Orson Welles, who interviewed me for a part in an unspecified movie. The interview turned out to be one of the most powerful and electric experiences of my life.

When I arrived at Orson's Melrose Avenue office, his secretary ushered me into a small room. Behind a rather small desk sat an enormously fat man exuding an energy I'd never before encountered. This was before he spoke a word. When that glorious voice rolled out, I became a dishrag. The interview went well (when I was able to speak), but the project never materialized.

Orson had sex appeal galore. And, flashing forward, so did another star I met, only socially this time, at a charity golf tournament: Burt Lancaster. He had an extremely seductive personality. The way he stood, the way he talked to you, the way he looked right into your soul with those black-lashed eyes of his—he was one of the sexiest men I've ever met, and a lovely, nice human being.

Let me do a Jeannie blink back to the past again. After I'd done a series of small parts in a series of not particularly distinguished movies, Wilt Melnick called and told me that, thanks to Mark Robson, Twentieth Century Fox was considering putting me under contract.

I was over the moon. I was living in the Studio Club just like Marilyn Monroe once had, and now I had been offered a contract by her very own studio, Twentieth Century Fox. But, as they say, it

*

never rains but it pours, because in his next breath he told me that *I Love Lucy* wanted me for a cameo as Diana Jordan in the episode "Country Club Dance."

The episode centered around a country club dinner dance at which Ricky, Fred, and a number of other husbands are too bored and complacent to dance with their middle-aged wives. A visiting cousin, the much younger Diana, sashays onto the scene and the husbands all vie for her attention and compete to see who will dance with her first. Diana picks Ricky and dances with him while the other husbands jostle to be next. Meanwhile, the wives watch, incensed.

While the script has them restore the balance the following day, when the wives turn on their own glamour and beguile their husbands at last, the plotline was a little too close to real life for my comfort.

Everyone loved Lucille Ball, but there was no doubt whatsoever that Desi Arnaz was a world-class philanderer. It was common knowledge in Hollywood that he had a taste for young, curvaceous blondes and that Lucy was deeply unhappy about Desi's infidelity. Worse still, he was blatant about his activities, and once even publicly boasted, "A real man should have as many girls as he has hairs on his head."

Now, I'm not a prude, but as far as I've always been concerned, married men are completely out of bounds to me. I made up my mind then and there that no matter how handsome Desi might be (and he was extremely handsome), no matter how persuasive (and with that Latin-lover charm, I had no doubt at all that he would be), I wouldn't succumb to his romantic blandishments. I wouldn't cause any trouble or hurt Lucy in any way.

Besides—and this has always been true throughout my career—when I work, I don't play. I focus single-mindedly on my role and won't allow anything or anyone to distract me from it. Usually that's very easy, but not on *I Love Lucy*, where Desi seemed to pop up wherever I was during rehearsal.

My solution? To hide from him whenever I saw him coming. Not a particularly subtle ploy, I know, but I was unable to come up with anything more effective.

During rehearsal, Lucy took me aside and said, "You're good, Barbara. You don't usually find a pretty girl who can project and be funny at the same time. But make sure to put that pretty little face of yours out there. Let the camera love your face. Don't look away from it."

That was Lucy. So different from Ann Sothern, and generous almost to a fault to a younger actress.

The day of the final shoot, I locked my dressing room door, put on my dress for the show (a nice if not particularly flattering number), and then tiptoed out, hoping against hope that Desi wasn't around and waiting to pounce on me.

Instead, I bumped straight into Lucy's assistant, who informed me that Lucy wanted to see me in her trailer dressing room at once.

Oh boy! I thought. *Have I done something to make her mad?*

I knew I hadn't done anything wrong, but I was still petrified. I followed the assistant into the trailer, where Lucy ordered, "Take that dress off."

Literally trembling from head to foot in fear, I did what she told me.

Then she handed me another dress.

Remembering Ann Sothern, I looked at it and thought, *Probably a sack dress.*

Then I put it on. It was the tightest, sexiest dress I'd ever seen, one that showed off all of my curves.

"Take it off again," Lucy said.

*

I did, and she and one of her friends spent more than an hour adding sparkles all over the dress so that it would look even more shiny and glamorous.

Now that's the kind of woman Lucille Ball was. She was really smart and really dedicated to her show, and even though she realized that Desi was actively pursuing me, she still put me in that dress because she knew it was right for the character and right for the show. The show meant everything to her, more, even, than her hurt pride over her cheating husband.

Even to this day in Hollywood, you still hear stories about how Desi broke Lucy's heart, but she still put her show first because she was smart and she was a professional.

Funnily enough, when I finally filmed the scene in which Desi and I dance together, he turned out to be a complete gentleman on camera and kept his distance from me. I was vastly relieved.

Afterward, the director took me aside and said, "You know, every time we have a young girl in the show and Desi goes after her, Lucy suffers so much. You were the first one who handled things professionally. Thank you."

Lucy also obliquely thanked me for evading her husband's advances: she offered to put me under contract for her new production company, Desilu. By then, though, it was too late. Twentieth Century Fox had finalized their offer for me to become one of their contract players, and it was far too good for me to turn down: seven years at $200 a week. I was on my way to making it in Hollywood at last!

*

chapter 4

TWENTIETH
CENTURY FOX

* * * * * * * * * * * * * * *

WHEN I FIRST arrived at the Twentieth Century Fox studios, I instinctively gravitated toward the warehouse in which the wardrobe department resided, where the costumes worn by Betty Grable and Alice Faye, actresses now long gone from the studio, still hung with their names stitched inside them.

I spent hours wandering through the wardrobe department, asking questions about the clothes and the stars who once wore them, and, in the process, became increasingly aware of the fleeting quality of Hollywood and of stardom, and of the ever-present potential for tragedy inherent in both.

Jayne Mansfield, who starred in *Will Success Spoil Rock Hunter?*, was a classic example (although I had no contact with her when I worked on the movie). Young, beautiful, sweet-natured, and far more intelligent than she was given credit for by the public and the press, she was to meet her death in a gruesome car accident. It seemed to me that her life story epitomized the quintessential Hollywood tragedy.

Then there was Debbie Reynolds, to whose "Aba Daba Honeymoon" Solly Hoffman and I had mimed. At the studio she was often on the telephone, issuing orders to the staff at her home. Very grand, I thought, secretly envying her and her happy marriage to Eddie Fisher. I could not know that Debbie's idyllic-seeming marriage would soon be shattered when Eddie left her because he had fallen head over heels in love with Elizabeth Taylor.

Elizabeth was signed to MGM (although she did make *Cleopatra* at Twentieth Century Fox, and there would be a ripple effect with consequences for me and my nascent career), and when I met her years later, I could hardly talk because I was so stunned by her beauty. Joan Collins was another great MGM beauty. Many years later, when composer Leslie Bricusse and his wife, Evie, invited my current husband, Jon, and me to their home in Acapulco, there was Joan by the pool, swathed in a white caftan, wearing a white turban, reclining on a chaise longue. Jon took one look at her and went, "Oh my God, she's so beautiful!" I wasn't amused by my husband's unadulterated enthusiasm for Joan Collins and snapped, "That's quite enough of that, Jon."

A Jeannie blink back to the past again: During my first few months at Fox, I experienced my fair share of disappointments. The first involved Mark Robson, my mentor and the man who had discovered me and brought me to Fox in the first place. Mark wanted me to read for the part of Betty in *Peyton Place*, which was projected to be a mammoth box office hit. I was elated at the prospect.

I was sent for wardrobe tests, a sure indication that the part was in the bag for me. Then Terry Moore, who had been in *Mighty Joe Young* and *Come Back Little Sheba* and had been involved with Howard Hughes, and who had initially turned the role down, changed her mind and accepted it after all.

I was bitterly disappointed, but fortunately, I didn't have too long to wallow in my disappointment. Just weeks later, I finally got my first big chance at Twentieth Century Fox after all: I was cast in the TV version of *How to Marry a Millionaire,* the movie that had starred Marilyn Monroe and Lauren Bacall.

TV again!

However, when I learned that I would be playing the part of Loco, one of the three husband-hunting Manhattan bachelorettes, which Marilyn Monroe had played in the movie version, I mentally tipped my hat to Emma Nelson Sims and her hitherto wacky-sounding predictions. It was a star-making role if ever there was one.

At first I was a little intimidated by the thought of following in Marilyn's footsteps, but then I gave the part more consideration and played Loco as being shortsighted. So that while I didn't want to banish the image of Marilyn's Loco completely from my mind while I was playing the part, I felt as if I'd stumbled on my own personal take on the character and was glad.

In the future, Marilyn would play a more significant role in my life than I had originally anticipated. And during *How to Marry a Millionaire,* our lives would intersect in a rather uncanny way, the significance of which I wasn't aware of until long after Marilyn's death, when her personal life became public knowledge.

I very much enjoyed playing Loco, and the series was a success. In November 1957, the producers of *How to Marry a Millionaire* sent me, Merry Anders, and Lori Nelson, the two other bachelorettes, to Manhattan to promote the series. As it was winter and the temperatures had plunged, they thoughtfully rented a full-length mink coat for each of us.

At the end of the tour, I was at Idlewild (as John F. Kennedy International Airport was then known), waiting for my flight to be called and about to buy some candy, when a dark, heavyset man sidled up to me and abruptly asked me whom I was with.

Startled, I said, "Booker McClay." Booker was Twentieth Century Fox's head of public relations.

The man strode off without another word. A few years later, I saw his picture in a magazine. The caption read, "Pierre Salinger."

Back at the airport, just as I was paying for my candy, Booker came over to me and asked, "Barbara, would you like to meet Senator John Kennedy?"

I wasn't in the least bit interested in politics, and the name Kennedy meant nothing to me at that time. But I didn't want to insult Booker, Senator Kennedy, or the man who'd approached me in the first place, so I shrugged and said, "Fine."

The heavyset man ushered me into an anteroom. Only a drumroll was missing, or a battery of klieg lights, as he declared in a loud ringmaster's voice, "I want you to meet the next president of the United States!"

Senator Kennedy was handsome enough to rival any Hollywood star. When he clasped my hand firmly, I looked up into the clearest, most hypnotic eyes in the universe. I blushed and looked away.

At that moment, fate intervened and my flight was called. I shook hands with the senator again. Then Pierre Salinger escorted me to the foot of the gangway.

As I boarded the plane in the ice-cold air, I tucked my hands into my pockets, and felt something in the left one. I pulled out a small piece of gray notepaper. Written on it were the initials "JFK" and a phone number.

Without any hesitation, I tore it up on the spot and handed the pieces to the stewardess to put in the trash.

I never once regretted it. The truth is that I wasn't even momentarily tempted by one of the most glamorous, charismatic, sexually alluring men who ever lived.

For I'd already met the man of my dreams. And nothing and no one, not even John F. Kennedy in his glittering prime, ever would have succeeded in leading me astray, because I was wildly, utterly, and completely enthralled by my very own Mr. Right, Michael Ansara.

*   *   *

As far as I—and thousands of fans and love-struck female fans throughout the world—was concerned, Michael Ansara was a magnificent specimen of alpha-male masculinity. Six foot four and darkly handsome, with blazing brown eyes, a deep, resonant voice, and a powerful aura of strength and dependability, Michael was a Hollywood heartthrob with sex appeal to burn.

He was born in Lebanon but came to America with his parents when he was two years old. He grew up in New England, where he lived until he was twelve. Initially he had wanted to become a doctor, but the theater beckoned, and he joined the Pasadena Playhouse, where his fellow students included Charles Bronson (who was to become a close friend), Aaron Spelling of *Dynasty* and *Beverly Hills 90210* fame, and sultry brunette actress Carolyn Jones. Down the line, with his dark, strong good looks, Michael would frequently be typecast in biblical epics, and he appeared in *The Ten Commandments*, *The Greatest Story Ever Told*, and *The Robe*. Ironically, the first time I saw him on the screen, in *Julius Caesar*, he aroused my interest only because he had the same last name as my first boyfriend, Al Ansara.

In October 1957, a month before I met Senator Kennedy, *How to Marry a Millionaire* was rising in popularity and I now had top billing on the show. I'd even managed to move out of the Studio Club and into an apartment of my very own on Sunset.

*

One morning, Booker McClay called me into his office and in no uncertain terms told me that it was high time I stopped hanging out with my boyfriend, Tony, a nice guy who delivered refrigerators for a living, and went out on the town with someone important in the business, so I'd see and be seen.

Before I could protest, Booker went on, "Barbara, you're in a hit series. You're a TV star. You get fan mail every week. Those fans expect you to be seen around Hollywood on the arm of a sexy date, and so do I."

I stifled a yawn.

I suppose I could have used my relationship with Tony as an excuse for not wanting to play the Hollywood social game, but that wasn't true. From the first, I'd made it clear to Tony that I didn't plan on going steady with him and that I was going to date other people.

I did meet actor Robert Vaughn at the Studio Club and go on one date with him. He was studying at UCLA at the time and was working extremely hard, but there was no chemistry between us and we never went out again.

Since then, Tony had suited me just fine and I wasn't remotely interested in dating another actor. But Booker just wouldn't take no for an answer. He insisted that I go to astrologer Carroll Righter's birthday party on Halloween as the date of Michael Ansara, one of Twentieth Century Fox's major stars, who was playing Apache chief Cochise to great acclaim in the TV hit *Broken Arrow.*

Tony or no Tony, the prospect of a blind date with some actor utterly underwhelmed me.

Michael, it later turned out, felt exactly the same way at the thought of meeting me. His exact words to Booker were "Why should I go out with some actress I don't know when I've already got so many girls in my life that I do know?"

But Booker was relentless, the date was set, and I was left wondering whether I ought to bone up on the Chiracahua Apaches and their current problems. In short, I expected Michael to arrive for our date sporting a shoulder-length bob and carrying a bow and arrow, just as he did in *Broken Arrow*.

Booker arranged for Michael and me to first have dinner at the Tail of the Cock, a restaurant on La Cienega, then to go on to the Halloween party, where photographers (who'd been tipped off in advance) would be waiting to grab a shot of us together. Mission accomplished, Booker McClay style.

However, things didn't go according to Booker's plan. From the moment Michael and I sat down to dinner, we didn't stop talking. We talked and talked and talked and talked, and practically closed the restaurant. We never did make it to the Halloween party, so Booker's photographers didn't get their pictures, and he was livid with both of us.

But Michael and I didn't care. We were far too busy falling madly and hopelessly in love.

Soon after, I left for Manhattan on the *How to Marry a Millionaire* publicity tour. While I was away, Michael called me every night, and our relationship deepened.

By the time I left Manhattan to return to Los Angeles, I knew that Michael Ansara was the man for me, that I wouldn't be dating anyone else, that I wanted our relationship to be exclusive.

But Michael, a decisive man with very little self-doubt, wanted more. One afternoon, without any warning, he showed up on the *How to Marry a Millionaire* set. He kissed me, then held out a white paper bag.

"Oh, goody!" I said. "Candy!"

My mouth started watering. I foraged inside the bag for the candy, and pulled out a diamond engagement ring instead.

"I think it will fit," Michael said laconically.

It did. It fit perfectly. A metaphor, in more ways than one, for our relationship and, I hoped, our future together.

Nevertheless, I wasn't quite prepared to commit to marriage to Michael then and there. My mother's advice not to go steady too soon or marry too young still held sway over me. So I hesitated in accepting Michael's proposal.

Meanwhile, Tony had somehow found out about Michael and had gone berserk when I refused to see him anymore. He called me constantly, waylaid me at the studio, and became so menacing that I was forced to ask the security guards at the gate to stop him from entering the lot.

I've never scared easily (not even when I had a death threat further along in my career, which I'll tell you about later), but Tony was totally out of control and I was terrified.

One night Michael and I were snuggled up on the couch in my apartment when the telephone rang. I picked it up and heard Tony's voice, muffled but instantly recognizable.

"Goodbye, Barbara. Goodbye," he said in a slurred voice, and hung up.

Within minutes, Michael and I were speeding over to the Highlands, the apartment complex where Tony lived. As we approached his apartment, we could already smell the gas.

Michael, ever a man of action, smashed through a window and climbed in, and I followed.

Inside the apartment, Tony was on the sofa, unconscious. Gas was pouring out of the oven. I grabbed a cloth, pressed it against my nose and mouth, and switched the gas off, while Michael dragged Tony outside to safety. An ambulance raced him to the hospital. To our great relief, Tony ultimately survived his suicide attempt.

But from that night on, I viewed Michael with new respect. He had stood by me in the midst of a crisis. He hadn't panicked, but had been there for me, a rock. He was strong, dependable, and gorgeous, but he was also eminently decent. Above all, he was a good man, and I hadn't met many of those in Hollywood. The town was full of boys trying to be agents and boys trying to be actors, but no real men. Michael was and is a real man.

Right after Tony's attempted suicide, I accepted Michael's marriage proposal. We were so in love, so eager to be married and spend the rest of our lives together, and we couldn't wait to tell our nearest and dearest the wonderful news.

Naturally, I expected all our friends and family to be happy that Michael and I were getting married, and in particular Booker McClay, the Cupid who'd introduced us to each other in the first place.

To my surprise, when I broke the news to Booker, he was less than enthusiastic about my marrying Michael.

A few days passed, then he sent word that he wanted to see me in his office again. He didn't beat around the bush. "Barbara, we—the studio—think you ought to wait a while before marrying Michael," he said.

Wait? This from the man who'd set up our first date? I was dumbstruck.

"You see, Barbara, we don't think you realize how many women hang around Michael on the *Broken Arrow* set each day. Women are flooding into Hollywood on Greyhound buses from all over the country hoping against hope to see him. He's surrounded by women who are crazy about him," Booker said grimly

I drew myself up to my full height. (Not that impressive when you are only five foot three, but you get the picture.)

"That's lovely," I retorted loftily. "Because I don't want someone whom nobody else wants!"

Now it was Booker's turn to be dumbstruck.

That night Michael and I set our wedding date for six weeks later.

Neither of us dreamed that Booker's negative reaction to our plan to marry was just the tip of the Twentieth Century Fox iceberg. Afterward, we found out that the studio honchos were distraught at the prospect of us marrying.

Their reaction was based on the fact that I was currently the youngest girl whom Fox had under contract; they hadn't even planted any items in any columns yet about me dating anyone, and now I was already talking marriage! Worse still, the sponsors of *Broken Arrow* were extremely worried that if Michael married me, his megawatt appeal to legions of women throughout America would instantly dissipate.

None of that bothered either of us, of course, and we just went ahead and booked the church, irrespective of anyone's objections. Naturally, we invited Booker to be our best man, and, to his credit, he accepted.

Now that the date was set, I discovered that I didn't have a thing to wear to my own wedding. But as I was basically working ten hours a day on *How to Marry a Millionaire,* I hardly had any time to scout around for the perfect wedding dress. To my delight, Mary Tate, the show's wardrobe mistress, came to my rescue and took me shopping for one. The only dress that I really liked was a white shantung silk suit that was about four sizes too large for me. Luckily, Mary arranged for the wardrobe department to cut it down to size so that it fitted me perfectly.

Next, my aunt Margie jumped in and lent me a hat, so that took care of something borrowed. A bigger problem, though, was how to stop my mother and her friend Elinor Hoffman—the kind and generous lady who'd given me the $100 that paid for my studies at the conservatory—from crying all the time. They weren't crying for happiness, either—they both thought I was too young to get married.

Michael and I held our ground and brushed aside everyone's objections to our union. We married on January 17, 1958, at St. Nicholas Greek Orthodox Church. Afterward, my aunt and uncle held a small reception for thirty guests.

Our wedding took place on a Friday. The following morning, I was scheduled to pose for publicity pictures. On Sunday, both Michael and I had to memorize our scripts in time for Monday morning, when we had to report to work on adjoining sound stages at Fox. So much for a honeymoon!

We moved into a duplex apartment off Sunset. I decorated the entire place in cream, and we were thrilled when Elinor Hoffman presented us with a precious miniature cream-colored poodle to match. We named her Maggie. We both loved Maggie and loved our home, but we weren't particularly domestic—though Michael cooked chicken once, his first and his last home-cooked meal. In the main, we thrived on TV dinners, books, conversation, and the powerful electricity generated by our brand-new love.

We were the very model of Hollywood actors—our careers were paramount, though we both wanted to have a child two years down the line. But I was still appearing in *How to Marry a Millionaire*, which went on to run for fifty-two episodes over two years, and Michael was still in *Broken Arrow*. Parenthood would have to wait.

Meanwhile, we were consolidating our finances. When I started working on *How to Marry a Millionaire*, the studio didn't increase my $200 weekly salary. However, Michael, always my biggest and most vociferous champion, and a man with an excellent head for business, argued persuasively that it wasn't fair for me to work twelve hours a day—and in sky-high heels at that—and not have my salary augmented. So Wilt stepped in and made a great deal for me whereby Fox paid me an extra $1,500 a week over my contract salary, then a king's ransom. Which was just as well, because later in 1958, after a total of seventy-two episodes over two years, *Broken Arrow* was canceled. We had no warning; the series was extremely popular, as was Michael, who was now a household name, and the cancellation was a big shock for both of us. The downturn in our finances was not particularly easy to manage, but fortunately, both Michael and I had a natural tendency toward thrift. However, our finances were once again battered after *How to Marry a Millionaire* was canceled in 1959. I went back to being a Fox contract player again, and my salary was back to my original $200 a week.

I might have started feeling a bit despondent if Wilt hadn't called with a wonderful offer: a part in *Flaming Star,* a cowboy movie starring Elvis Presley, the hottest male sex symbol in the universe. I'd first seen Elvis on *The Ed Sullivan Show* after my mother excitedly called me and insisted that I had to switch on the television and watch his performance. I did and was struck by his intense star quality and sex appeal.

In the movie, Elvis played Pacer Burton, the son of an Indian mother (Dolores del Rio) and a white father, born in Texas and torn between opposing worlds. Frank Sinatra and Marlon Brando were originally cast in the parts that Elvis and Steve Forrest would eventually play, but they backed out. Elvis had liked the script and thought the role a good one to play for his comeback after two years with the U.S. Army in Germany.

My role in the movie was originally cast with actress Barbara Steele, but at the last moment her accent was judged to be too British for the part. I was to play Ros, a rough-and-ready cowgirl who wore trousers and kept her hair in a long braid. I found it refreshing not to have to fuss so much about my clothes, hair, and makeup in the movie.

Elvis and I first met when preproduction of *Flaming Star* began on August 1, 1960. Shooting was scheduled to begin on August 16 at the Canejo Movie Ranch in Thousand Oaks. Exteriors were to be shot in Utah.

By now, I'd met countless stars, but the prospect of meeting the great Elvis Presley and working alongside him was still daunting. Luckily for me, he happened to be a big fan of Michael's—he loved *Broken Arrow* and in particular the character of Cochise—so that broke the ice between us.

I was surprised that Elvis even knew Michael, and I asked him how he'd managed to catch *Broken Arrow,* given his frenetic work schedule. He told me that he couldn't leave his hotel room at night for fear of being mobbed, so he stayed locked inside and watched TV for most of the night. That answer afforded me a poignant insight into Elvis's world, one that surprised me.

It was immediately clear to me, though, that Elvis cared passionately about acting and that he had his heart set on *Flaming Star* becoming a critical as well as a commercial success.

Before shooting began, Elvis had two weeks of riding lessons. He was the star of the movie, so I didn't question why no one suggested I have riding lessons as well. Surprising, really, in light of what happened next.

By the time shooting began on August 16, Elvis could ride extremely well, whereas I had never ridden a horse before in my life. Although a couple of ranchers gave me one basic lesson, I was happy when the wrangler assured me that they would be using a stunt double for any scenes in which my character was supposed to be riding a horse.

There was one particular scene in which Steve Forrest was at the top of a hill on his horse and my stunt double was supposed to ride up the hill screaming out my lines. However, at the very last

*

moment she was nowhere to be found, and without giving me any advance warning, the wrangler put me on the horse after all.

"Don't worry, the horse knows what to do," was all he said, and off the horse galloped up the hill, with me hanging on for dear life.

To my horror, I saw that we were heading straight for an irrigation ditch. My heart was pounding so loudly that I felt as if it were about to bust out of my chest, but to my everlasting relief, the horse made the jump.

I was just beginning to relax when my horse suddenly reared and then raced straight toward a tree with a great big hanging limb that swung threateningly in the wind.

"Duck!" yelled the wrangler.

I ducked, just in the nick of time.

As I did, the director blared, "Say your line, Barbara, say your line!"

Shaking from head to foot, I blurted out the line. Then the horse was off again, racing down the hill, while I hung on for dear life. Finally he skidded to a halt at the bottom. I was about to scramble down, when the director roared, "We'll do another take!"

I did just that, while Elvis stood and applauded.

*   *   *

It only took a couple of seconds with Elvis for me to recognize that he was really just a nice southern boy who had been taught by his momma to mind his manners and say please and thank you, just as I'd been taught to do by mine.

In fact, Elvis was far less flamboyant and far more low-key than Colonel Tom Parker, his manager and the man who'd discovered him. The Colonel roared onto the set every day in his big convertible

Cadillac. Swaggering around in his white suit and ten-gallon hat and puffing on a big cigar, Colonel Parker was definitely one of a kind, a maverick with no inhibitions and, some said, no scruples, either.

As for me, I rather liked the Colonel, because he never disguised who or what he was, nor how venal his motivations actually were. Bizarre as it may have seemed to all the rest of us on the movie, each morning the Colonel came onto the sound stage and set up a table on which he displayed Elvis's records, as well as books and magazines featuring him. I don't think anyone bought a single item, but the Colonel remained cool and unflustered.

As Elvis confided to me on the set of *Flaming Star*, "You know, Barbara, people say that I should leave the Colonel, but if it weren't for him, I'd still be that kid playing in a little bar down in Memphis. I know he's getting a big cut out of what I make, but he deserves every cent of it."

That comment was typical of Elvis: open, honest, and revealing. In between shots, we had similar intimate conversations on all sorts of subjects.

Elvis needed to have family and close friends around him for most of the shoot because he was fundamentally insecure. His father, Vernon, was usually on the set with him; it was obvious that Elvis loved his daddy and they were very easy with each other. He also had a group of guys with him at all times—his "cousins," as he introduced them to me. We all used to sit outside on the set and shoot the breeze together.

Years after Elvis's death, when I was on *Larry King Live*, one of the cousins called in. By then I knew that none of the guys I'd met all those years ago were related to Elvis at all, so I took the call, laughed, and said, "You stinkers! I honestly thought you all really were his cousins, but you're not!"

Elvis also confided in me about his new love, Priscilla Beaulieu,

*

an army colonel's daughter who was only fourteen when they met while he was stationed in Germany. Subtle as always, he broached the subject delicately by asking how Michael and I managed our marriage when one of us was away on location. "How do you handle being married to a man other women like so much, Barbara?" Of course, he was thinking of Priscilla and whether or not she would be able to cope with the armies of female fans forever pursuing him. I did my best to reassure him that so far, I had been able to rise above any jealousies or insecurities I might have because Michael was so damned attractive to legions of women.

But Elvis was still concerned.

"I'm really worried that she's too young," he said.

Time, of course, would prove him right, because when Priscilla grew up, she would ultimately leave him. But all that was years in the future, as was his gargantuan weight gain.

I'd been on a diet for what seemed like my entire life. I routinely ate coffee, toast, and grapefruit for breakfast, a meat patty and a boiled egg for lunch, and a salad for dinner. But despite my meager diet, my battle against putting on weight was ongoing, and I told Elvis as much.

"I've got to watch what I eat, because I'm like my momma and she and I always gain weight. So I have to be real careful," he acknowledged.

His mother had died two years before, and Elvis clearly venerated her memory. Family meant everything to him, and when he found out that my younger sister, Alison, was one of his biggest fans, he sent her a signed photo inscribed with the words "I'm glad to hear there's another one like her at home."

I was flattered. But while I adored Elvis, my heart belonged to Michael. As for Elvis, he was always courteous and respectful to me at all times, and there was never any suggestion that he harbored thoughts of putting our relationship on a less-than-professional footing. Not a glimmer. He was such a good actor.

It was clear to me during our time working together that he was achingly serious about making a success of the movie and about honing his craft. There was a great deal of honesty in his performance in *Flaming Star,* and it saddens me to think of how much better an actor Elvis might have become had the Colonel managed his career differently and made better artistic decisions on his behalf. In my opinion, Elvis could have become a really fine actor, but instead he became a superstar, an icon.

During the seventies, when he was headlining at the Las Vegas Hilton and I was married to my second husband, Chuck Fegert, Chuck and I saw Elvis's show there and went backstage to see him afterward.

Decades had passed since *Flaming Star,* but somehow I still nurtured the faint hope that Elvis might have retained the same southern-boy sweetness he'd once had. Sadly, I discovered that he was no longer the slim young man I remembered, but he was still using those southern manners with me.

In the dressing room, he took one look at Chuck and said bluntly, "I wanna know just how you got her. She wouldn't have anything to do with *me!*"

It had never occurred to me, all those years ago when Elvis and I worked together on *Flaming Star,* that he had any romantic designs on me, and I was shocked. He had been such a gentleman, but was that just a cover for his true intentions? All that vulnerability and self-disclosure—was it genuine, or was I still hopelessly naive and Elvis had just been using a cynical ploy to seduce me?

Thinking back to George Schlatter's revelation about Elvis's request after he saw me at Ciro's, I think I know the answer.

One final coda to my time with Elvis, and a tragic one at that:

*

When I was doing my nightclub act in Reno, during the seventies, I came down with a terrible cold. The show booker was most sympathetic and offered to take me to what he described as "a very special doctor," provided I promise that I'd only see him this once. Far too sick to question the booker's odd warning, I agreed and went to see the doctor, who prescribed some pills and gave me a shot.

The next morning, my cold had completely vanished. Delighted, I noted the doctor's number, in case I might need it the next time I played Reno. Then I remembered my promise to the booker.

"Why don't you want me to consult that doctor again?" I asked.

The booker hesitated, then finally said, "Well, Barbara, we had Elvis up here last month and he's not well. He has people around him who don't care about him as a person, but only care about him working, no matter how bad he feels, no matter how sick he is," he said.

I flashed back to *Flaming Star* and a conversation Elvis and I had had about work. *I love it, Barbara. Give me a guitar and I'm happy,* he'd said.

"So what did the doctor do to Elvis so that he could keep on working?" I asked the booker.

He hesitated again. "Elvis's butt looked like a pincushion. It had so many needle marks in it," he said at last.

The thought of my beautiful, handsome, gentlemanly Elvis in that condition was almost too much to bear.

A classic Jeannie photograph.

A baby picture taken of me at a Tuscon photo gallery, along with a rabbit; not mine. At the end of the shoot, I accidentally sat on the poor rabbit!

Me at three, dressed, as always, in plaid, on an outing in El Paso with my two grandmothers. A day I shall never forget, as I had my first taste of pink lemonade along with a homemade sugar cookie.

This photograph of me trying to look happy with a black patch over my eye was taken in front of our house on Ocean Avenue, San Francisco. My dog, Spotty, is beside me.

The Miss California beauty pageant, 1951. I am the third from the right in the top row, and not thrilled to be there. The girl who became Miss California is second from the right on the bottom row. I wasn't disappointed that I didn't win and was voted Miss Congeniality.

This photograph was taken for an album cover that I got after spotting the advertisement on that famous notice board at the Studio Club.

Sunning myself in a leopard-print bikini with my cream poodle, Maggie.

A classic Fox publicity shot.

My dance with Desi Arnaz, and as close as we were ever to get, despite Desi chasing me around the studio in an attempt to get ever closer.

A publicity still from the TV series *How to Marry a Millionaire*. My character, Loco, is reading a comic (difficult, as my shortsightedness is a running gag on the show). Lori Nelson is in the middle, and Merry Anders on the right.

A serious moment from *Flaming Star,* which matched the seriousness of Elvis's approach to his acting craft and the importance of my own commitment to my marriage vows to Michael Ansara, despite such temptations as Elvis and Paul Newman.

My scene with Paul Newman in *From the Terrace.* Paul Newman confided in me that he was delighted to be working with an actress he could look down on. Meanwhile, I was rigid with nerves at being so close to the impossibly handsome Mr. Newman.

A still from *The Wonderful World of the Brothers Grimm,* with me looking demure. When we were on location in Germany, my colorful co-star, Laurence Harvey, convinced me to have the most unpalatable meal of my life!

Voyage to the Bottom of the Sea was one of the few movies in which my first husband, Michael Ansara, appeared with me. That's him in the wet suit, along with Joan Fontaine and Robert Sterling.

A lighter moment with Clint Eastwood on the set of *Rawhide*. I didn't know that I was pregnant with Matthew at the time.

A posed shot from *All Hands on Deck* just before I gave Pat Boone his first on-camera kiss.

A publicity photograph for *The Brass Bottle*, with my amusing co-star, Tony Randall, and the less-than-well-behaved Burl Ives, who played a djinn with magical powers.

* * * * * * *chapter 5* * * * * * *

HOLLYWOOD STAR

* * * * * * * * * * * * * *

WHEN I WAS cast in *Flaming Star,* I wasn't remotely nervous at the thought of meeting Elvis, but on the day that my stand-in, Evie Moriarty, announced, "My other star wants to meet you," and led me onto the *Something's Got to Give* sound stage to introduce me to Marilyn Monroe, my nervousness knew no bounds.

Like millions of Americans, I loved and admired the screen siren. But through Evie, I also knew the woman behind all the glamour and the glitter. Evie, a beautiful blonde with large blue eyes and endless legs, never gossiped about the stars for whom she acted as a stand-in. But then Evie was much closer to me than she was to most people.

She and I went way back to *How to Marry a Millionaire,* when she had first doubled for me, and we had become friends. Our friendship was cemented when Michael was away on location and she stayed overnight at our apartment to keep me company.

Evie was fun, sassy; she knew and understood show business, and helped me get through the lonely evenings when Michael was working far away and I felt isolated and abandoned. Luckily, Michael approved of Evie, and the three of us had a running joke that she was "babysitting" me in his absence.

Beneath her Kewpie doll looks and showgirl glamour, Evie was relatively down-to-earth. For many years she'd been the girlfriend of Carl Laemmle Jr., whose father founded Universal Studios. She'd often turn up at the studio, her wrists weighed down with bracelets and her fingers with rings.

"Aw, Barbara," she'd say, "just look at what Junior gave me last night! What in heaven's name am I going to do with them? I never wear diamonds." Then she'd roll her big blue eyes up to the sky in mock distress.

She was so pretty, and a born actress, that I always wondered why she hadn't pursued a Hollywood career. She definitely had the looks, the sex appeal, and, of course, the contacts.

Her answer was invariably to screw up her pretty face and go, "Oh, Barbara, I can't even walk a straight line. And I can't walk and talk at the same time, either!" Subject closed.

The topic of Marilyn, however, was an ongoing discussion between us. Evie knew how much Marilyn fascinated me, and that I was one of the few people in town she could open up to without fear of what she said ending up in *Hollywood Confidential.*

Marilyn aroused such a sense of protectiveness in Evie that she watched over Marilyn as fiercely as a lioness might over a fragile cub. And she didn't mince her words when it came to anyone she thought was exploiting Marilyn or might be a danger to her in any way.

"People just aren't nice to her. She's insecure, they know it, and they build on it. Like that Strasberg woman, her acting teacher. She hangs around Marilyn like some kinda albatross," she said in a voice full of scorn. "And poor Marilyn is so petrified of not being a good enough actress that between scenes, she lies down on her couch and says her lines over and over and over again, so she won't make a mistake. They could all reassure her. But they won't, because it suits them not to."

Another time she told me: "Everybody is crazy about Marilyn's body, but Marilyn, she says she'd rather look like Kate Hepburn—boyish, not round. I keep telling her that she wouldn't be Marilyn if she looked like that, but she says she wouldn't care."

As time went on, Evie's revelations about Marilyn grew darker, especially in the months leading up to my meeting with Marilyn on the set of *Something's Got to Give:* hints that Marilyn had told her that she was being followed night and day, something about a man in a green Mercedes, her phone being tapped, even death threats.

By the spring of 1962, Evie was deeply worried about her "other star." At the time, Evie was standing in for me on *Five Weeks in a Balloon,* on which shooting was already under way. I sensed that there was trouble ahead when she came clattering along the corridor in her impossibly high heels, much faster than usual, a clacking urgency echoing in her footsteps.

"Barbara, Marilyn needs me. I'm gonna have to leave your movie early," she said.

Marilyn was the queen of Twentieth Century Fox. Evie was my friend. So I did my best to handle the news with as much grace as I was capable of mustering.

"Well, that's fine, Evie. When does Marilyn start shooting?" I said.

"Tomorrow," Evie said.

I must have looked a little startled, because she put her arm around me. "Barbara, honey, you don't understand. Marilyn *needs* me right now. You're a strong girl. You don't *need* me."

I wasn't going to admit it to Evie or put pressure on her not to leave me in the lurch, but in fact I *did* need her. She was my friend and my stand-in, the only one I'd ever had, and so I was filled with trepidation at the prospect of not having her stand in for me on *Five Weeks in a Balloon.* But I wasn't going to make things difficult for Evie, particularly if Marilyn needed her even more than I did.

As if she could read my thoughts, Evie went on, "Marilyn really *does* need me, Barbara. More than I can tell you."

I told her I understood, and she thanked me. The next time I saw her, on April 10, 1962, she was pulling me onto the *Something's Got to Give* sound stage because Marilyn had suddenly announced that she wanted to meet me.

So there I was in my clown outfit, complete with baggy plaid pants, about to be presented to the most glamorous woman on the planet. All I needed was a red nose and a dunce's cap for my humiliation to be complete. But Marilyn wanted to meet me, and both my curiosity and the good manners my mother had drilled into me held me back from refusing.

So I let Evie drag me over to sound stage 14, where I waited with her in the shadows for Marilyn to appear. Judging by the tension on the set and Marilyn's reputation for tardiness, everyone had been waiting for her for an inordinately long time. But no one complained. In fact, no one said a word. The air was electric with expectation, the stage quiet as a crypt.

Then Marilyn made her entrance: elegant, beautiful, vulnerable, wearing a black suit (the same one she wore in *Let's Make Love,* which costume designer Jean Louis thought might be suitable for her to wear in *Something's Got to Give* as well) and black pumps (which I knew were Ferragamo because afterward Evie nagged, "Barbara, you gotta buy them, they're perfect for you").

To me that day, everything about Marilyn was perfect, and for a moment I was rooted to the spot, almost paralyzed by anticipation.

She floated toward me, breathed the words, "Oh, oh, Barbara, it's so nice to meet you," and took my hand.

She really did talk like that. All air.

"Oh, Barbara, oh, Evie has told me so much," she breathed again.

Almost tongue-tied, I eventually managed to blurt out, "Yes, Evie babysits me."

Marilyn completely misunderstood and, to my embarrassment, said, "Oh, you have to come to the set again. And next time, do bring the kids."

I said I would.

There had been a wistful note in her voice when she said "kids," which is why I didn't explain or contradict her. Later, Evie told me how much Marilyn had longed to have kids, and how tragic it was that she never could.

That day, as I left the *Something's Got to Give* set, dazzled as I was by Marilyn and glad to have met her, however briefly, I also felt profoundly sad for her.

A few weeks later, she was dead.

Evie called me up in tears.

"She was so frightened, Barbara," she sobbed. "The hang-up calls. The man in the green Mercedes following her all the time. She knew who was behind it all, and why. She told me so. And now they're saying she killed herself. She would never have done that. Never, never, never. She may have been afraid, but she liked life, she liked life."

I have no doubt whatsoever that Evie was right on all counts.

* * *

After *Flaming Star* (which wasn't a big success, primarily because Elvis only sang one song in it, and that was recorded only after feedback from preview audiences who were scandalized that their idol wasn't singing in the movie) and the other movies that followed, I became unhappy at Fox. I tried to get the studio to loan me out to other studios, but they refused. So I remained at Fox, at the studio's beck and call, just waiting for someone to give me work.

When Mark Robson, the director to whom I owed my Fox contract in the first place, approached me and asked me to do a part in *From the Terrace*, I read the script and initially refused because my character—good-time girl Clemmie Shreve—only appeared in the film for one minute and eighteen seconds.

My scene, short as it was, took place at a party, where, as "You Make Me Feel So Young" played in the background, Clemmie sees Alfred Eaton (played by Paul Newman) across a crowded room, goes straight up to him, and says coquettishly, "Are you looking for me?"

"I am, if your name is Lex Porter," Paul says wryly.

"Well, my name is Clemmie Shreve, but I'll change it if it'll stop you from looking further," I say.

"How far am I allowed to look?" Paul says with a flirtatious glance.

Then I laugh a tinkling laugh and say, "I like you," and put my arms around him. "Sam?" I say.

"No, Alfred," Paul says.

I give him a flirtatious look.

"Are you going to make a pass at me, Alfred?"

"You believe in long courtships, don't you!" Paul says sardonically.

"Who's got the time? I'm crowding nineteen," I say.

"What, years or guys?" Paul cracks.

"Nasty," I say, and mash up to him. "Come on, let's dance and crowd each other."

Paul pulls away from me.

"I've got a wooden leg. I've got to fill it," he says.

"You mean it's over between us?" I say archly.

"These things don't last forever," Paul says abruptly, then extricates himself and walks away.

I stand there dejected for a moment, then straighten up and set my sights on another target.

A cameo, to say the least.

But Mark Robson had asked me to trust him and to accept the part, so I decided to do just that, primarily because I felt I owed him a debt. So I agreed to play Clemmie Shreve in *From the Terrace*.

My initial reward was that I got to wear a gorgeous blue-and-white gown that the brilliant fashion designer Billy Travilla created just for me. Billy designed the iconic cerise dress Marilyn wore in her "Diamonds Are a Girl's Best Friend" number in *Gentlemen Prefer Blondes,* and the gowns she wore in *The Seven Year Itch* and *River of No Return.*

My second was that I got to act a scene with Paul Newman. He had already made *Somebody Up There Likes Me,* had been nominated for an Academy Award for his bravura performance as Brick in *Cat on a Hot Tin Roof,* and was now one of the biggest male stars in Hollywood.

I was so in awe of him that at the last minute I almost changed my mind about appearing with him in *From the Terrace,* even briefly. I'd already signed the contract, though, so I had no option but to go ahead, scared stiff or not.

When I walked onto the set and, as my part called for, looked deep into Paul's eyes (they outdazzled even Jack Kennedy's), I was in Hollywood heaven. Paul must have been accustomed to evoking that reaction in besotted women, as he knew exactly how to put them at ease. He flashed me his hundred-watt smile and said, "Well, Barbara, you're the first actress I've ever been able to look down on."

He was trying to put me at ease, but he was also poking fun at himself. At the same time, his remark had a serious subtext to it—it wasn't just a gag designed to relax me. Although I didn't know it at the time, if the divine Paul Newman was insecure about anything about himself, it was his height.

How his height might have impacted Paul's star quality and his vast acting talent, I had no idea, but Paul obviously considered the negative rumors about his height to be destructive to his image. His height became such a big issue for him that when a New York newspaper described him as being just five foot eight, he erupted in fury and bet the newspaper that he'd write them a check for $500,000 if he was really five foot eight—and that they'd donate to a charity $100,000 for every inch of height over five foot eight that he could lay claim to. He was so intent on winning the bet that he even contemplated consulting an orthopedic man regarding how he could make himself taller when the newspaper measured him. Luckily for him, they never followed up on the challenge, but Paul's height, or lack of it, would always be his overriding insecurity.

That aside, he was a very down-to-earth guy and a great actor, who loved his wife, Joanne Woodward, passionately.

I'd resisted being tempted by Elvis and ignored John F. Kennedy's invitation to call him, but the truth is that had I not been married to Michael and madly in love with him, I might have been seriously tempted by Paul Newman. But, clever woman that she is, Joanne Woodward starred in *From the Terrace* with him, was on set that day, and would be on most of his future movies.

Which reminds me of Elvis and his misgivings that Priscilla wouldn't be able to cope with his pull over other women, and Booker McClay's warnings to me when I wanted to marry Michael.

I've always steadfastly avoided worrying about the man in my life cheating on me with other women, because I've always firmly believed that worrying about my husband being tempted by other women simply takes too much time and uses too much of my energy. I'd rather devote that time and energy to loving him instead.

The truth is that no matter how happy a marriage between actors might be, there are always tremendous strains. For Michael and me, the primary strain lay in the frequency of our separations caused by our divergent careers. In fact, our separations were so frequent that in 1967 we spent just four months together, as one of us was always away on location.

Michael, who was always more self-contained than I was, may not have suffered so much during our protracted separations, but I certainly did. Recently I found a 1962 newspaper in which I talked about the sadness I felt whenever Michael had to go away for work.

"He says goodbye—and all of a sudden half of you is gone. You come home and the house seems so awfully big and empty. You find yourself looking around corners, listening for his voice and his footsteps. It's dreadful! I miss him mostly at night. I miss him dreadfully then," I said.

Even after we'd been married for over seven years, I still hated being parted from Michael when he went away on location. So whenever I had a break from filming whatever movie I was working on, I would jump on the next plane and join him wherever he was. Once I traveled to see him on location where he was taking part in a rodeo. Michael was a brilliant rider and gave the impression that he was at one with the horse. At this particular rodeo, like at all the others, he rode bareback, marvelously. Afterward, I had to leave, and I remember standing by the fence crying, I was so sad to be parted from him.

While we were apart, I often had to work with extremely

attractive men, but Michael was never jealous, even though some of them flirted shamelessly with me. My experience with Harry Belafonte was typical.

We met during the seventies, when I was rehearsing for an NBC special and he was working on an adjacent set. He would spend hours watching me onstage, and when I came off, he flirted with me in the most enchanting way. But, handsome and charming as he was, I was never tempted by him. I was too in love with Michael. Moreover, I was never flattered when a man flirted with me, and still am not, because I don't see it as a compliment, or even take it personally; it is just the nature of men to flirt.

My first major separation from Michael occurred because he had to go to New York to do a play and I couldn't go with him because I had just started making *Five Weeks in a Balloon,* with Red Buttons.

During the shoot, Red developed a little bit of a crush on me. He must have been in his forties, but he still looked like a kid, and I think he felt like one as well. When it came to me, he certainly behaved like a kid, but I made it clear that I was married and intended to stay that way.

Later on, after I'd convinced Red that romance between us was completely out of the question, he invited me to go to the premiere of *Hatari* with him. I missed Michael, and I felt that my relationship with Red was on an even enough keel for me to accept an invitation from him without worrying about any consequences.

Stupidly, I'd forgotten that Red had just filed for divorce, and that the press would have a field day if we were at the premiere together, which they did.

When Michael saw the pictures of me with Red in the newspapers, he acted as if he could hardly believe his eyes. There was nothing for him to be upset about, so I told him that of course I had been to the premiere with Red, but if I had planned to step out on him, I certainly wouldn't have done so in front of a barrage of press photographers. Michael laughed and said that he knew I wouldn't.

Five years into our marriage, we bought a large four-bedroom house in the San Fernando Valley, complete with a play area and a swimming pool with a fence around it. The fence was there for one reason and one reason only: so that our future child could play safely in the yard without fear of him falling into the pool and drowning.

That yet-to-be-born child was constantly at the forefront of our minds, yet all our friends felt that we were crazy to buy such a big house just for the two of us, simply because we were dreaming of a family we might never have. For although we had been married for so long, it seemed that our chances of ever conceiving a child together were getting slimmer than ever.

* * *

Five Weeks in a Balloon marked the first time I worked with a lion (an experience I would reprise with Larry on *I Dream of Jeannie*). For some strange reason, this particular lion was permitted to roam free around the set, with his trainer standing by. Red and I were startled, but the trainer explained, "If you see him near you when he's out of the cage, don't move, don't run. He just wants to play with you, like a kitten plays with a ball of string, but no matter how playful he is, just remember that he is five hundred pounds of muscle and can really hurt you. And if he rolls over, don't move, because if you do, he'll break your legs."

Point taken—by me, at least. A few days later, during a break in shooting, Red and I, still dressed in our bright plaid pants from the movie, were having lunch on the grass at Lake Sherwood. Suddenly I looked over his shoulder, and there, a hundred feet behind Red, was the lion, prowling around, his tail switching.

"Don't move an inch, Red," I warned. "The lion's out."

Red almost jumped out of his skin.

"Where is it? Where is it?" he yelled at the top of his voice.

I glanced over his shoulder. The lion was now forty feet away, contemplating the two of us as if we might make a good lunchtime snack.

"Just stand still, Red. You know we're not supposed to move!" I said.

Whereupon Red flung himself between me and the lion, as if to protect me, and started leaping up and down and screaming, "To hell with that! To hell with that!"

At that moment, thank heavens, the trainer raced up to the lion and yanked him away from us.

So the poor lion missed snacking on two actors in bright costumes, and Red and I narrowly escaped certain death.

About the same time as I made *Five Weeks in a Balloon,* Fox loaned me out to MGM for *The Wonderful World of the Brothers Grimm,* co-starring Claire Bloom and Laurence Harvey. Laurence, who later would be much acclaimed for his tour de force in *The Manchurian Candidate,* exuded style and sex appeal and was a classic bon vivant. When we were on location in a little medieval village in Germany, he actually had his magnificent white Bentley shipped over there because he missed it so much.

The villagers, who'd never seen a movie star before, never mind a dashing one driving a great big Bentley, watched with their eyes popping out of their heads as Laurence roared over the quaint cobbled streets in his car, bound for some gourmet restaurant he'd somehow managed to discover in the area.

*

Usually I tagged along with our makeup artist in tow. One time Laurence insisted on taking us to his favorite restaurant, which he loved because, as he put it, "They make the best steak tartare in the world, Barbara, darling. You haven't lived till you've tried it."

I gulped, then came clean and admitted that I didn't eat anything raw, let alone raw meat.

Laurence blithely brushed my objections aside and commanded the maitre d' to prepare the steak tartare at our table. As he did, I fought back my desire to puke. Laurence, breezily unaware of my battle, gushed away at me happily—"Here you go, Barbara, darling. Sheer nectar"—and shoved a forkload of what I considered to be raw hamburger straight into my mouth.

I made a credible show of enjoying the steak tartare, but it was a miracle that I made it back to the hotel without throwing up every single bit of it all over Laurence's precious white Bentley!

I had much more fun when I worked on *Voyage to the Bottom of the Sea*, which I made at Fox with Joan Fontaine, Walter Pidgeon, and Peter Lorre of *Casablanca* fame.

Both Peter Lorre and Walter Pidgeon were already way into their sixties when we started shooting, but each of them was still flirtatious and entertaining. I had lunch with them in the commissary every day, and they were so cute with each other and with me that I really relished being in their company. Walter was a real Casanova and would wink at me and say, "Barbara, my dear, if you'd been around when I was younger, you wouldn't have stood a chance." Peter had a little bit of the devil in him, along with great kindness, and every inch of him laughed when he laughed. But when he wasn't laughing, he gave me excellent career advice, including one particular gem: "Barbara, no matter how successful you become, always sign your own checks. I didn't—I let my business manager sign them on my behalf—and that's why I'm still working today."

Later, I discovered that Peter had hired a close friend to be his business manager, primarily because he wanted to concentrate on acting and not be bothered by mundane tasks like paying the window cleaner. He had implicitly trusted that friend with his wife, his child, his life, and his money. But the friend had robbed him blind, and Peter was now practically penniless.

That didn't stop him from fighting over the check with Walter every day and insisting on paying for my lunch. When I protested, Peter said, "Not only are you a young, pretty girl, but you're a contract player as well, so you can't pay for lunch." Before one lunch with Peter and Walter, I took the waiter aside and tried to slip him some cash for our lunch, but he categorically refused to take it. Mr. Lorre and Mr. Pidgeon had made a deal with him, he said; Miss Eden must never be allowed to pick up the check.

When I had one last try and challenged Peter and Walter to let me pay the check, they had a fit. Peter was practically down to his last penny, but he still paid for my lunch, that day and every other day during the shoot.

They don't make 'em like that anymore.

After the fiasco of *Cleopatra,* Fox's extravaganza starring Elizabeth Taylor, Richard Burton, and Rex Harrison, which failed to ignite the box office sufficiently to justify the (then) stratospheric $44 million it cost to make, the studio underwent a dramatic change in fortunes and closed down. My last movie there was *The Yellow Canary,* with Pat Boone.

I was now free to make movies for whichever studio I wanted, and I was delighted. One of the positive consequences of leaving Fox was that in the future I would work at MGM, the cream of all the studios, where the hairdressers, makeup artists, and wardrobe staff were the best in the business, the costumes were hand-stitched, and endless care was taken in lighting actresses so they would look more beautiful on the screen than they did in real life.

Working at MGM was like going to an exclusive charm school, where actresses were taught every trick in the business to enhance and exploit their natural assets. An example: we were taught that, unlike brunette hair, blond hair always has to be smooth and blow-dried, otherwise it will look frizzy, as if it has been accidentally singed in a fire.

At MGM, we were taught to wear the same color hose as our shoes, to create the illusion of longer legs, and to wear pale nail polish to make short fingers look longer and more graceful. At MGM, I also learned to apply false eyelashes, and wore them there for the very first time, to great effect.

I worked at MGM with Tony Randall on *Seven Faces of Dr. Lao,* and canny Tony divined one of my weaknesses (other than ice cream and chocolate): gin rummy. As the movie included a lot of night shooting, between takes we would sit in my dressing room and play the game together.

Tony never lost a single game, and after a while I realized that he was winning a small fortune from me. So I started to watch him more closely. Then it dawned on me: he was sitting opposite a mirror that was reflecting my cards back to him. In other words, he'd been cheating, and how!

Tony and I never played gin rummy together again. Meanwhile, it swiftly transpired that he had other games on his mind, and seemed determined that I play them with him. I kept reminding him of Michael and my marriage, but Tony, a devil with women, was oblivious to all of that. He was a funny man, though, and all his approaches to me were couched in humor. So although they came to nothing, he made me laugh uproariously in the process, and I will always cherish his memory for that.

*

Married or not, I performed my fair share of love scenes during my Hollywood years, and in most of my movies invariably played girls who ended up being either kissed or rescued, and sometimes both.

One screen kiss I'll never forget was with Pat Boone, when we made *All Hands on Deck*. As the plot had it, our kiss was designed to be relatively chaste. But Pat had never before played a role that called for him to kiss his co-star. Consequently, while kissing Pat Boone on camera was just part of a day's work for me, to Pat, his first on-screen kiss was a major event.

It turned out that his wife and three daughters felt exactly the same, because just as the director was about to shout, "Action," they all trooped onto the set. A second before Pat and I first locked lips, I heard one of the little daughters whisper, "Watch out! Daddy's going to kiss someone who isn't Mommy!"

But *All Hands on Deck* wasn't always a barrel of laughs, primarily because the director, Norman Taurog, was a really, really mean man. He was child star Jackie Cooper's uncle, and when Jackie was a little boy acting in the movies, Norman was notorious for sticking a pin into him so that he'd cry real tears in a scene. During *All Hands on Deck,* Norman hollered at everybody, with the exception of Pat. On the rare occasions when Pat was late to the set, Norman would take it out on the crew, and on everybody else in the bargain. So we all hated him. And he continued to be so much of a bully that even Pat, who was a really nice, easygoing guy, grew to hate him in the end.

One morning Pat and I were doing a scene on the bow of a U.S. Navy ship. Norman was in an inflatable raft next to the ship, along with the cameraman filming the scene. All of a sudden, Pat and I heard a splash next to the ship. We looked down and saw that the raft with Norman on it was sinking. All of us just watched the raft slowly go down, and I'm afraid I couldn't stop myself from laughing. We were only just off Long Beach, so the water wasn't that deep.

I wasn't laughing much, though, on my next movie, *Brass Bottle,* with Burl Ives, in which Burl played a djinn, a genie. Working on *Brass Bottle* is probably my least favorite Hollywood memory. On the other hand, the movie would prove to be a good-luck charm for me: Sidney Sheldon saw it, it sparked the germ of *I Dream of Jeannie,* and he remembered my performance in it.

On the surface, Burl Ives was genial and kind. He was wonderful on the set, when other people were around, but at the end of the day, when it was dark, I didn't dare risk walking by his dressing room.

He'd stand by the door like a big bad bear and beckon: "Come here, little girl. Come here." Then he'd lunge straight at me. Luckily, I was quick enough on my feet to sidestep him, then I'd run like hell.

The first time it happened, I couldn't believe my eyes. This darling, warm Santa Claus of a man, who was in his mid-sixties (which, as far as I was concerned, seemed like a hundred and ten) was actually making a pass at me. Incredible!

* * *

Less incredible, but still intimidating, was Warren Beatty, who was filming *The Many Loves of Dobie Gillis* on the sound stage next to where I was shooting *How to Marry a Millionaire.* Whenever I was on my way to makeup, he'd loom out of the shadows and scare the living daylights out of me by whispering, "Barbara Eden! Barbara Eden! I'm gonna come and get you right now!"

I understand that this may sound very sappy, but I genuinely was still wet behind the ears, and so I really did find Warren to be dreadfully scary. I think that he sensed my naiveté and enjoyed the effect he had on me. Every time I'd see him about to spring out at me, I'd run a mile to avoid him.

I suppose that in some ways Warren was darling, but I always think that darling is as darling does. And, to be honest, I wasn't altogether sure what I'd do if he did eventually catch me, because I was so attracted to his physicality. My salvation, however, was that he didn't have the kind of qualities I generally look for in a man.

Not at the time, that is. I'll do a Jeannie blink forward twenty years or so: I'm between marriages and up for a part in a Warren Beatty production. Wardrobe and makeup have finished with me, and I'm now waiting in my trailer to be called to the set.

The trailer door swings open and there, in all his mature glory, is Warren. Without a word, he saunters up to me, kisses me on the lips, and then saunters straight out again.

I didn't get the part. Nor was the movie ever made. End of me and Warren. End of story. Cut.

chapter 6

GETTING
JEANNIE

★ ★ ★ ★ ★ ★ ★ ★ ★ ★ ★ ★ ★ ★ ★

JUST BEFORE *I Dream of Jeannie* swirled into my life like some kind of magical tornado, I did the TV series *Rawhide*. Clint Eastwood starred as Rowdy Yates and I appeared as Goldie, a dance hall hostess, in a two-part episode, "Damon's Road," which aired in November 1964, just before I began shooting *I Dream of Jeannie*.

My appearance on the show was a radical departure from *Rawhide*'s usual classic cowboy plot, as that episode had a musical comedy slant and included a fair bit of singing and dancing. Coincidentally, I had a short scene in that episode in which I wore a harem girl costume, virtually identical to the one I'd soon be wearing on *I Dream of Jeannie*.

However, *Rawhide*'s Goldie, in contrast with Jeannie, wasn't lighthearted or humorous in the least. To the tune of bizarre tinkling music, I appear onstage in my rather provocative harem costume and do a lot of solemn pouting, wiggling, and fluttering of my rather heavy eyelashes, while the audience of cowboys whoops and hollers. Then Clint rides into the arena on his horse and stops the show.

There was more, including a scene in which I sing "Ten Tiny Toes," but my *Rawhide* stint was really only interesting in that it brought me into close proximity with yet another male Hollywood sex symbol, Clint Eastwood.

Although I was unaware of it at the time, I was pregnant when I shot that two-part *Rawhide* episode. When my pregnancy was finally made public, Clint sent me a production still of myself as Goldie, inscribed with the words "And we never even knew you were pregnant."

Apart from having a good sense of humor, Clint was intensely attractive, already exuding a superstar glamour. Women flocked to him in droves. He was then married to his first wife, Maggie, but as he has publicly admitted in a *Playboy* interview, they conducted a somewhat open marriage. Nonetheless, whenever I saw Maggie Eastwood, I could tell that she was suffering dreadfully, particularly when Clint's primary girlfriend, Roxanne Tunis, a beautiful, statuesque stuntwoman, openly canoodled with him on the set.

Roxanne routinely sat on Clint's lap in full view of the cast and crew (many of whom knew Maggie and felt embarrassed for her). Roxanne was obviously a fixture in his life. She and Clint went on to have a child together, a daughter whom Clint has publicly acknowledged.

During the time we worked together on *Rawhide,* Clint enjoyed the attention of other girls as well, simply because they constantly offered themselves to him. Every inch a man, Clint was clearly flattered and didn't always refuse to engage with them romantically.

However, I still hadn't come up against any threats from other women to my marriage, no matter how young and beautiful they were. Despite the fact that Michael and I had been married for almost seven years, I was still secure in his love, and he in mine.

Looking back, I suppose part of my attraction for Michael lay in the fact that although I was an extremely hardworking actress, I remained the epitome of a classic early sixties wife, the kind who existed in the far-off era before women's liberation. Of my own volition, I even addressed Michael as "Daddy," and didn't feel in the least bit self-conscious or ashamed of it. However far women have come since those days, I still don't feel any need to apologize for how I related to my husband in the past. That's just how it was back then, old-fashioned though it may all seem now.

I guess Clint and Maggie were ahead of their time in having an open marriage. I'm not being judgmental, but that kind of marriage never would have worked for Michael and me. We were far too intertwined, far too devoted to each other. We were a team.

Talking of male-female teams reminds me of Fred Astaire and Ginger Rogers. In 1976, I made *The Amazing Dobermans* with Fred. He was seventy-seven at the time, sweet and self-effacing, and a consummate professional. There was no ego. He was doing an extremely small film, but he was quite happy to just sit around and wait for his call.

During a break, I mentioned how much I admired Ginger, and Fred said, "Oh, yes, feathers!"

"Feathers?" I asked, curious.

"Ginger was a great dancer," he said. "But she had a very dominant mother who decided which costumes she'd wear in the movies she made with me. Every time Ginger and I would dance, I'd sweat profusely, so the feathers on her gowns would get stuck on my face and on my arms. I was so irritated by all the feathers that I finally asked Ginger not to have feathers sewn on her costumes anymore."

"But she always wore feathers in all her movies!" I cut in.

"Exactly," said Fred with a small smile. "Her mother refused to allow her to leave the feathers off her costumes. And Ginger complied."

Fred Astaire was such a nice, gentle man, but with that anecdote he lifted the lid on the tensions simmering beneath the pristine surface of his legendary relationship with Ginger Rogers. They'd been a team, yes, but her mother clearly called the shots.

Another legendary star who came into my life briefly was Cary Grant, whom I met in the mid-sixties, shortly before I began working on *I Dream of Jeannie.*

As a challenge, I accepted a part in a stage musical, *The Pajama Game,* with John Raitt (now better known as Bonnie's father), but as I hadn't sung in public since singing with the band in San Francisco, shortly before the show opened I began to suffer an acute case of stage fright. Apart from my long absence from the theater, I also felt considerably hampered because the show was being put on in a theater in the round, and I'd never performed in that kind of venue before. I was petrified that I wouldn't be able to find my entrances or exits.

John Raitt was a fabulous actor with a great baritone voice, and he was also something of a ladies' man. But he was incredibly helpful and encouraging to me. Nonetheless, on opening night I was quaking in my shoes. To compound my terror, just before my entrance I stood backstage and peered into the audience, unable to make out any of the faces except one: Cary Grant's!

Cary Grant was in the audience with his future wife, Dyan Cannon. And I was sure that I was about to give the worst performance of my entire career right in front of one of the greatest Hollywood legends who'd ever lived. I felt as if I were about to be instantly dispatched straight to hell in a Hollywood handbasket, with no escape, no reprieve.

The band struck up my entrance music. The ground seemed to shift beneath me, and for a moment I thought I was about to faint. I considered making a break for it. But then common sense and a devil-may-care touch of recklessness kicked in out of the blue, and I told myself, *Go down there, Barbara Jean, and make a great big fool of yourself! Just do your best and let the chips fall where they may—as long as you don't fall flat on your face as well!*

With that, I stormed onstage and—holy mackerel!—I got through the show in one piece. I didn't make a complete and utter fool of myself, Cary Grant didn't storm out of the theater in disgust, and Dyan Cannon didn't split her sides in derision at my performance.

Instead, John Raitt invited me to join him, Cary, and Dyan for dinner. The consummate charmer and a quintessential English gentleman, Cary made my evening by being unfailingly kind to me and telling me over and over how wonderful I'd been in the show.

I knew he was lying through those perfect, gleaming teeth, but I didn't care. I felt so marvelous, so grand. And I'll always be grateful to Cary for making me feel that way.

However, my meeting with another Hollywood legend and one of Cary's most beloved co-stars, Katharine Hepburn, ended up playing out somewhat differently. During the early eighties, I was invited to see her in *West Side Waltz,* at Los Angeles's Ahmanson Theater. My date was Henry Wolltag, a very good-looking, tall, and elegant silver-haired British gentleman in his early sixties, with perfect manners.

She was predictably brilliant in the show, and I couldn't wait to go backstage and congratulate her afterward. I'd even hesitantly prepared a few things to say to her when we met, including Evie's revelation that Marilyn had longed to look like Katharine. I was pleased at the prospect of relaying the compliment to her.

So after the show, Henry and I went backstage to pay a call on Miss Hepburn. We were ushered into her dressing room. And I had hardly taken a breath, never mind uttered a single word to her, when she swept straight past me and right up to my dashing British beau, and started batting her eyelashes at him most fetchingly.

Soon they were engaged in animated conversation, while I stood there in the background, like a discarded store mannequin. There was just one second when Miss Hepburn deigned to throw me a cursory glance, then spun around and turned her back on me without a single word. I was dismissed, and how!

Clearly, Katharine Hepburn had no time whatsoever for attractive blondes. And I sincerely hoped that poor Marilyn had never met her in person, either, as she probably would have been most unhappy to be on the receiving end of Miss Hepburn's disdain. As for me, I chalked it all up to yet another tale in the saga of my encounters with Hollywood divas.

Lauren Bacall was another formidable Hollywood diva with whom I crossed paths when she was starring in *Applause* onstage in Los Angeles. My agent arranged for me to meet Lauren, as she was scheduled to take a break from the production and I was slated to replace her.

We met at the theater between shows and she looked me over briefly, with hardly a smile or a flash of warmth. I had expected to be fascinated and beguiled by her, but when I left her dressing room I was just saddled with the impression that she was large, commanding, and definitely in charge. I had no clue as to her impression of me, but guessed that it wasn't remotely positive.

My guess was confirmed when, the following morning, she contacted the producers of *Applause* and, for reasons not revealed to me afterward, informed them that she had now decided not to take a hiatus from the show after all. I wasn't altogether sorry, as *Applause* truly was Lauren Bacall's show and I was happy to keep it that way.

Hollywood is a far smaller town than people outside the business tend to realize, and—all that negative publicity about casting couches aside—a great many shows are cast by serendipity. *I Dream of Jeannie* was one of them.

Let's Jeannie-blink to the summer of 1964. Sure, I'd read about *I Dream of Jeannie* in the trade press, that it was a fantasy about a female genie, but there was nothing in the article about any bottle yet, or what kind of an actress the show's creator, writer, and producer, Sidney Sheldon, was planning to cast as his Jeannie. The word, though, through the grapevine, was that he and the show's producers were holding clandestine meetings with Miss Greece, Miss Israel, and other sultry five-foot-nine beauty queens with a view to auditioning them for the part.

I never dreamed that Sidney would consider me for the role of Jeannie. But then I didn't know that he'd seen *Brass Bottle,* or that we had a number of mutual friends who were comedy writers and seemed to like and admire my work.

So I almost passed out in shock (also partly ecstasy) when Sidney called me, unheralded, and announced, "I hear you are my Jeannie!"

I never did discover who suggested me for the part, but Sidney, of course, knew a good line when he had one, so—after I picked myself up from the floor—I still didn't assume that the part was mine. I believed that he was seeing a slew of other actresses far better suited to playing Jeannie than I was.

When I accepted Sidney's invitation to have tea with him at the Beverly Hills Hotel's Polo Lounge, I did so with very low expectations that anything would come of it. But I like very few things in life better than tea and cakes, preferably chocolate ones.

Let me pause to say a few words about the incomparable Sidney Sheldon, one of the most prolific and successful writers of all time. Born in Chicago, the son of a salesman, he attended eight different schools as a child, and discovered his writing talent when he was just twelve and he wrote, produced, directed, and starred in his very own mystery thriller.

After graduating from Northwestern University, he decamped

to Hollywood, where David O. Selznick hired him to vet a script for the princely sum of $3. After that, Darryl Zanuck hired him to read and analyze scripts for a slightly higher salary and on a more permanent basis, after which Sidney's career soared.

A brilliant, imaginative writer, he wrote the screenplays for a dazzling array of Hollywood classics, including *Easter Parade*, *Annie Get Your Gun* (along with Irving Berlin), *The Bachelor and the Bobby Soxer*, and TV's *The Patty Duke Show*. *I Dream of Jeannie*, his latest project, I knew from our mutual friends, was very close to his heart, and he totally believed in it.

So Sidney and I had tea together at the Beverly Hills Hotel, during which time he airily dismissed my doubts about not being a five-foot-nine dusky brunette from foreign climes, but rather a pint-sized, curvy American blonde. We chatted about comedy writers we'd both worked with, and life in general, and the hours sped by. At the end of our tea, I felt as if I'd made a wise new friend, but I still never imagined that Sidney would cast me as Jeannie.

So you could have knocked me down with a feather (shades of Ginger Rogers) when, just a few days later, Sidney called and said, "Congratulations; you are now officially my Jeannie!"

I was pleased to have gotten the job, but I didn't exactly jump up and down for joy. After all, I had no idea how the pilot would turn out or if it would be picked up by a network. Still, a job was a job, and I was determined to do my best.

I was then working flat out on *Rawhide* at Universal, so when Sidney called and asked me if Larry Hagman, one of the actors whom they were considering for the part of Captain Tony Nelson, could rehearse with me, I suggested that we rehearse in my dressing room at the studio during a break from *Rawhide*.

"Fine," Sidney said. "We know you can act, we know he can

act, but what we want to check out is whether or not the two of you have chemistry."

Now, chemistry between two people is something so magical, so indefinable, that not even the best actors can fake it, nor can the greatest director bring it out in them if it doesn't exist.

I knew very little about Larry except that he was Mary Martin's son, which really intrigued me, as my mother had always been a fan. From as far back as I could remember, she had always held Mary up to me as the perfect example of a brilliant singer and entertainer.

Born in Texas, the daughter of an attorney and a violin teacher, Mary Martin got her start in show business appearing on the radio in Dallas. She first made her mark in Cole Porter's *Leave It to Me*, in which she sang the showstopper "My Heart Belongs to Daddy." She went on to make ten movies for Paramount, and then skyrocketed to stardom when she was cast as Nellie Forbush in *South Pacific*, which went on to break Broadway box office records and then run in London for five blockbuster years.

Mary garnered yet more fame and fortune when she starred in *Peter Pan*, for which she won a Tony, then in *Annie Get Your Gun* and *The Sound of Music*, for which she won yet another Tony. Meanwhile, Larry was growing up in Texas, far removed from his mother, who had sent him to live with his grandmother when he was still a little boy.

Down the line, I learned that Larry had always resented his mother for putting him in Black Fox Military Academy when he was less than ten years old. (Even then, my mother sprang to Mary's defense and argued that Mary probably didn't have any other choice.) And when Mary Martin married Richard Halliday, who later became her manager, the young Larry had problems relating to him.

However, show business was in his blood, and nothing could

prevent him from pursuing it with a vengeance. Like his mother, Larry launched his acting career in Dallas, where he worked in the theater. Following that, he spent five years in the chorus of the London cast of *South Pacific,* in which he played a Seabee (a member of the construction battalion of the U.S. Navy), along with Sean Connery. Later, he joined the U.S. Air Force and was stationed in England, where he met and married Maj Axelsson, a Swedish fashion designer, and he remains married to her to this day, in one of show business's most enduring matches.

During his four years in the U.S. Air Force, Larry produced and directed shows for American airmen stationed in Europe. Then he moved to Manhattan, where he appeared in Broadway and off-Broadway plays, including *Once Around the Park, Career,* and *The Nervous Set.* After that he switched gears and moved on to television, where he found a home in the soap opera *The Edge of Night* and stayed on the show for two years.

Clearly destined for a bigger arena than daytime soaps, Larry struggled through nine months of unemployment, then finally won the part of Tony Nelson in *I Dream of Jeannie.* According to Sidney in his autobiography, *The Other Side of Me,* "Larry wanted to show the world that he could be as successful as his mother. The result was that he put himself and everyone else under tremendous pressure."

All that said, from our first meeting I was bowled over by Larry's charm and his talent as an actor. Sidney and the *I Dream of Jeannie* producers had wanted to ascertain whether or not Larry and I had chemistry together, and as soon as we began the scene, I had no doubt whatsoever that we did. Our acting rhythms were in synch, and the scene in which Captain Nelson and Jeannie first meet worked like a perfectly crafted, intricate piece of clockwork.

We both had exactly the same sense of timing, and the sparks between us invariably flew. Not that there was ever any kind of romance between us. If Warren Beatty, John F. Kennedy, and Tony Randall couldn't lead me astray, Larry Hagman certainly couldn't. Nor did he try. Besides, like Joanne Woodward, his wife, Maj, made sure to always stay close to the set.

Larry had been married to Maj for most of his adult life and wasn't particularly experienced with women. When I flung my arms around him there in the dressing room, just as the script called for me to do, I sensed him recoil slightly.

I was immediately hit with the realization that Larry was intrinsically shy with women. Much later, he admitted that I had been right. "That day in the dressing room, I thought to myself, *Here's this woman attacking me in her dressing room! What the hell am I getting into?*"

I was only playing my part exactly as it was written, but Larry was genuinely shocked. From that time on, though, the tables would be turned, and it would be Larry who would be doing all the shocking.

On the subject of shock, though: Before the pilot of *I Dream of Jeannie* was even made, the NBC censors stepped in and laid down the law with regard to what they considered would shock our audience. NBC executives had had a preview of the script and were horrified by what they considered to be a scandalous premise and an even more scandalous script. So on November 17, 1964, their Broadcast Standards department issued a list of stiff guidelines for the show.

However ridiculous the guidelines may seem from the perspective of today, as *TV Guide* pointed out, "*I Dream of Jeannie* is actually one of the most daring shows on TV. It is the only show, for example, in which an attractive unmarried girl has the free run of a bachelor's apartment." And as far as NBC was concerned, the matter of Jeannie and morality had to be taken extremely seriously in the show—as seriously as if she were a real-life woman and the story we were telling was fact, not a figment of Sidney's deliciously over-wrought imagination.

NBC's vigilance, as difficult as it may be for anyone who wasn't around in the early sixties to understand, was not unusual. For example, in the case of *The Smothers Brothers Comedy Hour,* on which I once played a sex education teacher, the network censor cut the word "sex" from the script.

This is what NBC decreed so as to preserve the moral tone of *I Dream of Jeannie:* (1) It was imperative that my harem trousers be lined with silk so my legs didn't show through the transparent fabric. (2) Jeannie's smoke was banned from disappearing under Captain Nelson's bedroom door. When the series was up and running and some of the episodes had been shot but not aired, the NBC censor went crazy about one particular episode, and we had to reshoot it because, as he solemnly declared, "The smoke must never spend the night in the bedroom of a man." From then on, if the smoke representing Jeannie ever went under the bedroom door, it had to be seen to come out again, otherwise the audience might assume that the smoke—aka Jeannie—was still in there, a definite no-no. (3) Openmouthed kissing between Tony and his fiancée, Melissa, was banned. (4) Nor was Jeannie permitted to be provocative or flirtatious. As Broadcast Standards phrased it, "Avoid the seductive and sexual innuendos when Jeannie says, 'And I am going to please thee very much.' It would be helpful here to have her mention some specific pleasures such as jewels or money."

I never considered Jeannie to be provocative or flirtatious, by the way, because I always thought of her as a tomboy, not a vamp.

During the run-up to the pilot, I was involved in countless discussions regarding Jeannie's hair, makeup, and clothes. Celebrated Academy Award–winning costume designer Gwen Wakelin created the harem outfit that I wore in the first season, although toward the very end of the season, on my suggestion, whenever it was appropriate, Jeannie graduated to wearing ball gowns and other more conventional clothes. I also picked the color pink, my favorite color, for the harem outfit, although the color didn't really matter at all in the first season, as it was shot in black and white.

At that time, most TV shows were already being shot in color, but because the executives behind *I Dream of Jeannie* didn't want to spend the $400 extra per episode, the first season was scheduled to be shot in black and white. Sidney was so outraged that he offered to invest his own money in having the show shot in color, but the executives still refused to budge.

Sidney also was kind enough and democratic enough to ask me to select which color I wanted the inside of the bottle to be, and I picked purple, my other favorite color. In fact, at the time, I loved purple so much that my dressing room was decorated in purple—purple walls, purple carpet, purple everything.

Gwen designed my iconic hairstyle by creating a ponytail with a braid secured around it, topped by a circle of velvet through which my ponytail was pulled to give it height.

Director Gene Nelson came up with the idea of Jeannie's blink, but I realized that it wasn't a strong enough gesture, so that's when I got my ponytail going, and added a nod as a way of signaling a flashback or a flash-forward in time.

In every episode of *I Dream of Jeannie,* although the audience might not have realized it at the time, I kept a little bit of home—of Michael—close to my heart by wearing the one-carat diamond pendant he'd given me on a chain around my neck. Michael and I had bought it downtown in a wholesale jewelry mart because I wanted one so badly, and wearing it helped me feel close to him. My *I Dream of Jeannie* diamond wasn't an especially high-quality diamond, but I still have it. And it meant a lot to me that Sidney and the producers gave me the go-ahead to wear it during *I Dream of Jeannie.*

Yet although my input was sought regarding Jeannie's style and wardrobe, I had no illusions that the show belonged to anyone other than Sidney, who had created it and would be writing and producing every single episode.

Larry Hagman, however, was not so sure. When he got the part of Captain Nelson in the pilot, he swung into action to exercise as much control over the show as he could. He appeared in 80 percent of the pilot and every episode that followed, and later he was paid $150,000 a year for the role—peanuts in comparison to the megabucks today's TV stars get paid, but an enormous sum in those days. Larry was set on *I Dream of Jeannie* making him a star. In a way, you could hardly have blamed him, as even before we started shooting, the magnitude of his role really did seem to merit those great expectations. That hope would fuel his actions right from the start of filming the pilot.

That was fine by me, and I genuinely hoped that Larry would satisfy his heartfelt ambitions, but as soon as I studied the script in detail, it became clear to me that Sidney had written it in such a way that the character of Captain (later Major) Nelson would play straight man to my Jeannie. It was in truth a thankless role, and Larry would kick against it every step of the way (much more on this later).

Even on the first day of shooting the pilot on Zuma Beach, Larry made no bones about the fact that he despised the script. Consequently, he decided to ad-lib whenever possible, which drove the director, Gene Nelson, completely crazy.

Gene, a former actor and now an experienced and well-respected director who had directed *The Donna Reed Show* (then a big hit) and *The Farmer's Daughter*, with Loretta Young, initially bore the brunt of Larry's rebellious nature.

Without much provocation, Larry was consistently temperamental and confrontational. Most of the time it seemed like he was spoiling for a fight. He was driven by the conviction that the show would be a big hit. Plus he was a perfectionist par excellence and wanted to get the pilot right.

At first, Larry's need for control didn't trouble me one bit. I was far too focused on the show and on making Jeannie a memorable character. In countless interviews, journalists have asked me how much of Barbara Eden there is in Jeannie, but the truth is this: none. I played Jeannie as Sidney wrote her, and if I infused anything into my portrayal of her, it was as a result of asking myself how it would feel to be catapulted into another world about which you know nothing and to come face-to-face with automobiles and appliances, objects you've never heard of or seen before.

I gave Jeannie's relationship with Captain Nelson an equal amount of consideration. Clearly she had never had a boyfriend, and when suddenly this gorgeous man materializes in front of her, she is almost terrified. I say "almost" because I always felt that Jeannie was innately wise. Wise, but nevertheless still a fish out of water, in the great American movie tradition that embraces both Dorothy in *The Wizard of Oz* and Mr. Smith in *Mr. Smith Goes to Washington*.

That first day at Zuma Beach, however, the weather proved to be my biggest problem. It was freezing, and there I was in my pink chiffon costume, shivering on the beach, while Larry was snug as a bug in his NASA uniform and all the rest of the crew were swaddled in wool and cashmere.

Toward the end of the day, I had become literally blue with cold, and was immensely grateful to the crew for offering me a glass of brandy—my first—which warmed me for a time but didn't take the edge off the cold completely.

I soldiered on as best as possible, hoping against hope that Gene Nelson would call it a day. Cold as I was, I still took great pains to properly enunciate the Persian dialect I'd been taught by a UCLA professor whom Sidney had hired for the purpose (although later on, for some reason, they switched Jeannie's mother tongue to Babylonian).

I was just inwardly congratulating myself for having succeeded, when all of a sudden a gargantuan wave hammered me. I almost lost my balance, and was soaked to the skin. I didn't give a fig about that, though I was aware that the wave had been big enough to seriously injure me.

Apart from Larry's outburst in the car on the way back home from Zuma Beach, the first day passed without further incident. We shot the rest of the pilot at the Columbia studio on Gower, where, despite being cocooned in the safety of a sound stage, life wouldn't always be easy.

We were scheduled to shoot a scene in Captain Nelson's apartment during which I was supposed to jump in the air and land on the sofa next to him. Relaxed and happy to do the scene, I blithely executed my jump, only to hit my head on Larry's knee and crack my tooth. Blood flowed everywhere, but Larry was very, very sweet to me, as were the rest of the cast and crew.

We wrapped the pilot without any further incident. And as it transpired, it would end up being my favorite *I Dream of Jeannie* episode of them all.

After we shot the pilot, the producers, Screen Gems, showed it to selected audiences, and word came back that I had tested higher for approval than anyone else had ever tested.

****** *chapter 7* ******

I DREAM OF
MATTHEW

* * * * * * * * * * * * * * *

BY THE FALL of 1964, the only tension in my marriage to Michael was our failure to have children together. Then one day in the fall, when I was in the middle of filming a guest shot in an episode of *Slattery's People,* in which I was playing the first love interest Richard Crenna had on the show, I suddenly felt extremely nauseous.

I had a love scene to film with Richard, but I felt like I was coming down with the flu, and was now faced with a real dilemma. I had a quick internal debate with myself about whether to kiss Richard or not, thinking, *Poor man, if I kiss him, he's bound to get the flu from me. But if I tell the director and refuse to do the scene, they'll have to stop shooting, which will cost the producers a great deal of money. Plus the rest of the cast and crew will have to stop working as well.*

Hoping against hope that Richard, a healthy-looking specimen of a man, was in possession of a strong immune system, I held my breath and kissed him as best I could.

Over the next few days, I felt as if I were a zombie. I was tired and listless. I dosed myself with all sorts of remedies, but when everything failed, I went to see my doctor.

"This being-on-the-verge-of-having-the-flu-but-not-having-it is for the birds," I said plaintively. "I just want to stop it in its tracks or have it and get it over with. Couldn't you give me a shot of something that will bring it out of me right away?"

My doctor looked at me, perturbed. "I think I'll give you some tests, Barbara," he said finally.

Alarm bells rang in my head. "Tests?" I said.

"Pregnancy," the doctor said.

"Pregnancy? We've been trying to get pregnant for seven years! There's not a snowball's chance of me being pregnant after all that time," I said when I'd stopped laughing.

Ignoring my laughter, the doctor did indeed give me a pregnancy test, and following that he tested me for other serious illnesses as well. Afterward, I went home and slept for what seemed like months.

Two days later, Michael and I were delighted when we got the news that NBC had picked up the *I Dream of Jeannie* pilot and had committed to Screen Gems making twenty-two episodes. We were just in the middle of a celebratory kiss when the phone rang again. My heart sank. *It was all a mistake,* I thought. Now that the series was a reality, Sidney had changed his mind and picked Gina Lollobrigida to play Jeannie instead!

Michael took the call. My fear turned to confusion as I watched him listen, then light up like a million-watt electric bulb.

"We're pregnant! We finally did it, honey!" he shouted.

We were overjoyed and clapped our hands like a pair of excited children.

Then, after the first flush of euphoria began to subside somewhat, we began to plan exactly how I would break the news of my pregnancy to Sidney, so that he could replace me in the show as quickly as possible.

We didn't for one second bemoan the bad timing of me getting a part in a new series and not being able to accept it because I was pregnant. After all, we'd been trying to conceive a child for almost seven years, and nothing was more important to us than that.

Besides, the concept of *I Dream of Jeannie* seemed flimsy, to say the least, and no one knew if the series would run for more than the initial twenty-two episodes that had been commissioned by the network.

But I liked and respected Sidney and knew it was imperative I tell him right away that I was no longer going to be his Jeannie, so that he could begin holding auditions for my replacement.

I plucked up my courage and called him at home. He answered the telephone after just one ring.

"Glad you caught me, Barbara. We were just going out to dinner," he said.

I took a deep breath. "Sidney, I need to see you right away. I've got something to tell you," I said.

"Tell me now," he said, a hint of impatience creeping into his voice.

"I can't, Sidney. I just can't," I said.

He must have sensed my urgency, because he agreed to see me at his host's house before dinner began.

Michael drove me there and waited in the car outside while I braced myself to face Sidney.

He gave me a warm smile—very few people I've ever known could smile as warmly as Sidney could—and in a moment that recalled Emma Nelson Sims and her uncanny psychic ability, he cracked, "Don't tell me, Barbara—you're pregnant!"

"Oh, yes, Sidney, yes, I am," I said, and practically threw my arms around his neck. "Isn't it just wonderful?"

Sidney, a class act to his fingertips, didn't chime in with, *Yes, but what about my show?*

I tore myself back to reality.

"I'm sorry to do that to you, Sidney, but I wanted to tell you right away so you'd have time to replace me," I said contritely.

Without a moment's hesitation, Sidney said, "You haven't done anything to me, Barbara. You're staying in the show."

"But—but how?" I stammered.

"Let me think about it, Barbara. I'll get back to you tomorrow."

The end result? Sidney came up with an almost foolproof technique for disguising my pregnancy by draping me with a multitude of veils and instructing that I be shot only from the waist up, or from a distance. Consequently, I worked on *I Dream of Jeannie* right up until the eighth month of my pregnancy, and filmed eleven episodes of the show during that time.

Before we started shooting one of the very early episodes, I arrived in my dressing room to discover that a red one-piece bathing suit had been laid out for me to wear in the episode. Horrified at the thought of being paraded on camera like an overstuffed elephant, I rushed straight to Gene Nelson's office and made it clear to him that I wouldn't wear the offending bathing suit under any circumstances.

"But Barbara, this isn't *you*," he said, shocked. "You're never temperamental!"

"I'm not temperamental, Gene," I said. "I'm pregnant."

Well, directors are directors because they are in the business of directing. And none of them relishes having his commands disobeyed by a lowly actor. So, in the most polite terms he could muster, Gene swept aside all my objections and repeated his request that I try on the bathing suit.

Confrontation has never been my forte, so I put on a brave face and capitulated, but under one stringent condition: there was no way on earth that I would step out on the set in that bathing suit for all the cast and crew to see. I would only put it on if Gene came to my dressing room and saw me in it there. Fully aware that I meant business, Gene agreed.

So I went back to my dressing room, squeezed myself into that damned bathing suit, put a robe over it, and then, when Gene arrived, flashed him.

Seeing that I had an obvious belly bump, he did a fast retreat.

"Okay, Barbara, you win. I'll come up with something that works for you," he said.

Ultimately, on his suggestion, I kept the bathing suit on, and walked out onto the set with a towel draped strategically around me.

This particular scene was to be shot beside a swimming pool. The ever-resourceful Gene had me lie down by the pool, put an inflatable swim tube around my bump, and cover myself up so that my pregnancy remained invisible.

In other scenes, he draped me in yards of chiffon veils, so I looked like a walking tent. Gene's inventive ways of disguising my pregnancy turned out to be magical, because neither the critics nor the viewers ever realized that their two-thousand-year-old Jeannie was expecting a baby.

During the first seven and a half months of my pregnancy, I scarcely put on a pound. Then, during the last few weeks, I packed the weight on dramatically. Everyone who saw me commented that I was going to have either twins or a very big baby indeed.

Gene Nelson's wife, Marilyn, threw a baby shower for me, and I received so many lovely gifts that we had to send for Michael to transport them home for me.

On August 29, 1965, less than a month before the premiere of *I Dream of Jeannie*, I woke up at two in the morning, wracked by excruciating pains. I didn't want to wake Michael, so I suffered in silence for as long as I could. Then at three-thirty, when the pain became unbearable, I woke him up. Within seconds, he had shot out of bed and called the doctor, and we were on our way to Good Samaritan Hospital.

Six hours later, we were still in the hospital's waiting room. Michael tried to stay calm, while in the vain hope that I might distract myself from the pain stabbing through me, I read a book, the title of which has long since escaped me.

When I finally went into the delivery room, Michael waited outside, pacing back and forth. Twelve hours after we arrived at the hospital, Matthew Michael Ansara, a big baby with dark eyes, long dark eyelashes, enviably thick dark hair, and a sweet smile, was born.

We called him our lucky-charm baby. We had a child at last, and we loved him more than words could say. Our joy was boundless, and our hopes that he would live a healthy and happy life were unlimited. Matthew meant everything to both of us, and always would.

He was just three weeks old when *I Dream of Jeannie* first saw the light of day. For a show that was destined to endure for 132 episodes over five seasons (and countless more times in reruns), when *I Dream of Jeannie* was first released, it didn't meet with much fanfare from the press.

In fact, no less an industry powerhouse than *Variety* carped, "Miss Eden plays a genie who materializes out of an Egyptian jug to badger an astronaut, making his commanding officers believe he's off his rocker, driving his fiancée up the wall, and teasing viewers with dirty minds with innuendo (like the climax of the initialer, what was happening behind the camera in astro boy's bedroom?)."

Down the line, when the feminist movement swept America, the critics also lambasted the show for depicting a master-slave relationship that they claimed was an insult to liberated women everywhere.

I always considered that to be nonsense. *I Dream of Jeannie* is a fantasy, a modern-day fairy tale that has nothing to do with women's liberation. The show's purpose was not to make a political statement but simply to entertain audiences, which is what it indisputably succeeded in doing.

I Dream of Jeannie genuinely delved into the battle of the sexes, but in a cute way. Jeannie truly believed that Captain Nelson was her master, that she was there to serve him. But she also loved him and believed that he didn't know what was good for him, *she* did. For despite the surface elements ("Yes, Master," and so on), it was Jeannie who dominated Major Nelson, not the reverse. She invariably got her way and liked it. And besides, what all the critics seemed to forget was that Jeannie wasn't a flesh-and-blood person but a fantasy. She simply didn't exist.

By the end of the first season, we all recognized that *I Dream of Jeannie* was a hit. Surprisingly enough, while the show was an unqualified success throughout the five seasons it aired, it was never an industry sweetheart. Yet audiences loved it and still do. And after all, *I Dream of Jeannie* has lasted far longer than many shows that won cartloads of Emmys and reams of accolades from the critics; over the long haul, that longevity is what counts.

When we began filming the second season of *I Dream of Jeannie*, Matthew was five months old. Consequently, while I was working, I spent most of my downtime dreaming not of Jeannie but of Matthew, wondering what he was doing, what he was eating, and how he was sleeping. I missed him from the bottom of my heart whenever I had to be parted from him.

When the show was on hiatus, I worked in summer stock all over the country, guested on other people's TV shows, and appeared in my nightclub act in Las Vegas and throughout the country. I worked so hard partly because I wanted to, but partly because after

Broken Arrow was canceled, Michael wasn't working as much as he used to, and although we were both frugal and had a cushion of savings, my income was more important to us than ever.

But it broke my heart when Matthew looked at me with those big brown eyes and said, "Mommy, why do you have to leave again?"

I tried to explain to him that everyone in the world had to work and that I was extremely lucky to be able to do work I loved, that I missed him very much when I was away, and that I'd always come back to him as quickly as I could. But while he understood on a rational level that I had to work, with hindsight I am afraid I have to admit that our separations probably hurt him on an emotional level.

One time I was in a play in Ohio when he came down with a terrible case of flu. The poor little boy was racked with fever, and Michael was out of his mind with worry. He did the best he could to take care of Matthew, but I knew that my son also desperately needed a mother's touch. I couldn't walk out of my job in midseason, so I sent a frantic SOS to my mother up in San Francisco. Mother, bless her, rose to the occasion: she threw some clothes into a suitcase and boarded the next plane to LA. Under her gentle and loving care, Matthew's health improved by leaps and bounds.

But I was so traumatized by not having been there when he was sick, then having to miss his second birthday because of a commitment in Las Vegas, that when Bob Hope invited me to entertain the troops at Christmas that same year, I reluctantly declined. My refusal may have seemed selfish to other people, but having missed Matthew's birthday, I was determined that I should not miss the first Christmas of his life when he was old enough to be aware of the holiday. I wanted to see him opening his gifts, and I'll always be grateful that I did.

In a way, Matthew grew up with Jeannie, in much the same way

Candice Bergen grew up with Charlie McCarthy, her ventriloquist father Edgar Bergen's celebrated dummy.

As soon as Matthew was able to talk, one of his first sentences was "Momma Jeannie!" enunciated when we perched him in front of the show. After a while, I realized that he was talking not about me at all but about the show. Other times, when he would watch the show (and he seemed to want to watch it all the time), he would point at the set and ask, "Where is Jeannie?"

I'd tell him, "I'll be on in a minute, honey."

His reaction? "Where is she?" Then, a little while later, while he watched a scene featuring only Larry and Hayden Rorke, he'd say, "Where are you, Mommy?" as if he expected me to be on the show every single second.

Soon I learned that other little children also believed implicitly that *I Dream of Jeannie* represented a slice of real life, and that Jeannie herself was a flesh-and-blood woman capable of making magic whenever and however she liked.

When Matthew was a little baby, I took him to the market, where he rode in a seat in my cart, and a little girl and her even smaller brother came up to us. The little girl was wearing her school uniform and seemed as meek and mild as an angel. All of a sudden she looked at me, pointed at her brother, and declared, "Turn him into a frog!" Her brother promptly burst into tears—and you could hardly have blamed him!

It wasn't too surprising, then, that as a child, Matthew always had such a difficult time distinguishing between illusion and reality, between what was happening on camera and what was happening off. When he was a year old, I took him to watch me guest on *The Mike Douglas Show*. In a gag that took place at the end of the show, Leonard Nimoy carried me off the set while I kicked, screamed, and protested vociferously. Watching on the greenroom monitor, little Matthew burst into floods of tears, and no amount of explaining that Mommy was fine and was only playacting would comfort him.

It would probably take a psychoanalyst to understand Matthew's inner thoughts, but it was understandable that seeing his mother on TV practically every night was more than a bit confusing for a little boy.

I had to prevent myself from advising him to "rise above it" when, as a very small boy, he went to nursery school and afterward complained, "The other children keep bugging me and asking me if I'm magic."

"So what do you say to them?" I said.

"I tell them, 'No, I'm not. *She* is,' " he said, somewhat proudly.

Such was the international appeal of the series that when I traveled to Hong Kong on a promotional tour for *I Dream of Jeannie* and was walking through the packed streets with some of the crew, I turned around to find a throng of Chinese people dogging our footsteps. I started to get frightened when I realized that every single one of them was staring at me. But the faster I walked, the faster they walked, and the more people who joined them. I was so unnerved that I whispered to one of the Chinese crew with me to try and find out what was going on, why they were following us.

Then a bold English-speaking Chinese lady pointed at me and came straight out with it. "Are you the magic lady?" she said.

"Sometimes," I replied.

In America, too, crowds followed me wherever I went. Flattering, but difficult if I wanted to spend a private day concentrating on Matthew and my family. My solution? To wear a red wig and hope no one would recognize me.

One time I was taking Matthew, then eight, to Disneyland, and invited my sister, Alison, and her four-year-old daughter, Michelle, to come with us. Beforehand, I put on my red wig and a pair of big dark-lensed glasses, and when we stood in line for tickets, I felt confident that no one in the park would recognize me.

No such luck. A perceptive young girl came running up to me, waving her autograph book, and eagerly asked, "Aren't you Barbara Eden?"

Shocked that my disguise had failed and my attempt at privacy had been foiled, I didn't think before blurting out, "No, I'm not."

Hearing me, little Michelle reacted with a horrified "Auntie Barbara lied! Auntie Barbara lied!" No matter how carefully we explained the situation to her, she never really understood it.

That day at Disneyland, the girl obviously didn't believe me, and alerted all her friends that Jeannie was standing in line. Subsequently, pandemonium broke out, and to Matthew's disgust, I had no alternative but to sign autographs, which I did with as much courtesy as I could muster. At which point the man running the ride spirited all of us—Alison, Michelle, Matthew, and me—to the front of the line.

"Sometimes it helps to be a genie," I said to Matthew with a wink.

As Matthew grew older, it was clear that he didn't much like being Jeannie's son. Moreover, by the time he was six or seven and the show was in reruns, he actively resented the show and my part in it.

He really didn't want to share me with anyone, and I didn't blame him. I did everything I could so that he would know he was the most important person in the world for me, that he was number one. That wasn't difficult, because he was a darling little boy, and everyone who met him immediately warmed to him. I took him on tour to the Persian Gulf when I was appearing there with Bob Hope, and when I did my show in Las Vegas, he would be there in the wings watching me rehearse.

I was proud and happy to have him there, and always basked in his love and admiration, the memory of which still sustains me today. One of my funniest memories of Matthew as a child goes back to the times when I was all dressed up and ready to go onstage in Las Vegas. Matthew, then about eleven, always clapped his hands and cried, "Oh, Mommy, you're so pretty!" which naturally warmed my heart. And whenever he saw a glamorous singer or actress on TV, he'd always comment, "Oh, Mommy, she's so pretty." He'd pause for a second, then without fail he'd add, "But not as pretty as you, Mommy."

Then one day we were watching TV together and Raquel Welch came on. Matthew exclaimed, "Oh, Mommy, she's so pretty."

I waited and waited, but that was it.

So I asked, "Prettier than me?"

And Matthew said, "Well . . ."

I fell down laughing.

On a more serious note, I never once doubted his deep and abiding love for me. When he reached his late teens and early twenties, Matthew became my greatest defender, a chivalrous knight in shining armor, loving and protective in the extreme.

During the late sixties, Tony Curtis and one of his daughters used to come up to the house and play Ping-Pong with me and Michael. After one or two desultory games during which Tony's mind, not to mention his body, seemed to be miles away, I realized that playing Ping-Pong wasn't the primary motive for his visit. He came to our house to smoke pot without his wife knowing about it, and that's what he'd done.

Along the way, Tony said something extremely inappropriate to me. Matthew happened to overhear every single word, and he went ballistic and threatened to deck Tony. I tried reasoning with him ("rise above it" and so on), but that didn't work with Matthew, and it was all I could do to stop him from avenging my wounded virtue and socking Tony Curtis in the jaw.

An international tabloid scandal concerning Matt and another household name was narrowly averted when, in 1992, I made an appearance on shock jock Howard Stern's radio show. It goes without saying that I wasn't keen to be on the show, but my manager asked me to do it, and I guess we had a movie to promote. So I gritted my teeth and sailed through the show, turning a deaf ear to some of the more salacious comments made during my brief stint.

Two minutes after we went off the air, I was in the midst of making my escape from the studio as quickly as was polite when I received a heated call from Matthew.

I hadn't warned him in advance that I was guesting on the show, because I hoped fervently that he'd never find out, but as chance would have it, he was driving his truck through the streets of Los Angeles at the exact moment when my interview went out over the air, and he heard every word of the segment.

I concentrated my energy on preventing Matthew from instantly heading to the studio, where Howard Stern was still on the air, and giving him hell for the way he'd treated me. Matthew was fit to be tied, and it was all I could do to convince him that it takes all sorts to make the world of entertainment go round.

When that failed, I resorted to taking the blame myself. "Howard Stern didn't force me to go on his show, Matt," I reasoned with him. "I went on it by choice. And I knew exactly what I was doing and what I was in for."

He still was far from happy. And it was only a couple of hours later, after I had recovered from my shock that he'd heard the show, that it finally occurred to me I should have had the presence of mind to quiz Matthew on what exactly *he* was doing listening to *The Howard Stern Show* in the first place!

However, I caught myself wishing that Matthew had been around the time when I was asked by a sports magazine to present an award to O. J. Simpson. The ceremony took place at Jack Lemmon's office on Beverly Drive. It was just another job to me, but out of respect to the magazine and to the event, I wanted to look my best, so I wore a peach chamois leather pantsuit to the ceremony.

From the moment I walked into the room, O.J. was all over me like a bad case of measles, flirting outrageously and making a series of suggestive remarks. I'm not unaccustomed to men speaking to me that way, but when they do, I somehow manage to tune them out. I did just that with O.J.

I posed for pictures with him, smiling as sunnily as I was able. Meanwhile, O.J. was ignoring everyone else in the room and just talking to me; he acted as if I were the award he'd been given. And although I tried to evade his advances as politely as possible, as luck would have it (or is it that old Murphy's law again?), a journalist on hand to report on the ceremony must have picked up on the underlying tension between us. In the article on the award ceremony, the journalist quipped acidly, "O.J. didn't seem to care much about the award. All he could see was Barbara."

It's true that O. J. Simpson did come on to me in an extremely blatant and aggressive way, but I did nothing to encourage him. Nevertheless, the journalist went so far as to unfairly blame me for having invited O.J.'s advances, simply because I was wearing tight pants. I was hurt and angry.

Sometime afterward, I was invited to Nicole Brown Simpson's birthday party and O.J. came up to me, all wide-eyed and innocent, and said, "Oh, Barbara, I hope I didn't upset you at that award ceremony. I hope I wasn't rude to you." Of course he did upset me, and of course he was rude. I merely shook my head and moved away from him. My mother would have been proud.

A few years later, I saw Nicole and the children at an airport and said hello to her. She looked very tired and was in the midst of telling the children, "We have to go and see Daddy now." I could tell that she was deeply unhappy.

*   *   *

Time for a Jeannie blink back to my *I Dream of Jeannie* years. Although I worked extremely hard, I was content, both in my own career and in my marriage to Michael. When we were shooting the show, I would get up at five every day, arrive at the studio for makeup at six, and work until seven in the evening. In those days, none of the cast went to dinner together afterward, or to a bar or a club. We just rushed straight home and studied our scripts in preparation for the next day's filming.

Now and again, however, Michael and I did make time to get together with friends like Steve and Neile McQueen, who lived in a small house in Bel Air, where we'd sometimes go to dinner. Later on, I was so shocked when Steve and Neile announced they were getting divorced, because when we were together it was so clear that they adored each other. After their divorce, we lost touch. Then some years later I was at Columbia Studios, heard someone calling my name, and turned around—and there was Steve!

He hadn't changed a bit. It was as if time had stood still. We had coffee together and laughed, joked, and reminisced about the past. Steve was a genuinely good human being, a kind friend, and I remember him with great affection.

Which brings me back to *I Dream of Jeannie,* the show with which I will always be associated, the show that consumed five years of my life. Even with the wild roller-coaster ride I had with my talented, iconoclastic drama king of a co-star, Larry Hagman, I wouldn't have had it any other way.

****** *chapter 8* ******

ALL ABOUT
LARRY

* * * * * * * * * * * * * *

THIS MAY BE one of the biggest understatements ever made, but for Larry Hagman, the *I Dream of Jeannie* years were not happy ones. To this day, I believe he much prefers to be remembered for his role as J. R. Ewing in *Dallas* rather than for his role as Major Tony Nelson in *I Dream of Jeannie.*

To be fair to Larry, he wasn't the cause of every single solitary drama out of all the many that unfolded on the *I Dream of Jeannie* set. One good example was during season three, while we were shooting "Genie, Genie, Who's Got the Genie," which aired on January 16, 1968. My mother visited the set for the very first time, and saw me locked into the interior of a safe, with only a gigantic lipstick and a purse for company.

All of a sudden, a flat from the set fell across the safe. Only quick thinking by a crew member saved me from being hit by it. We started the scene again, but then the lipstick toppled over and practically knocked me out.

My mother, watching, gave a big start and said, "Barbara, I never knew that making a TV series was so dangerous!" Of course she didn't. She hadn't witnessed Larry in full flight yet.

In his memoirs, Larry claimed not to be able to remember the *I*

Dream of Jeannie years, but I find that difficult to believe, given the high-octane quality of his explosive on-set shenanigans.

On one unforgettable occasion, when Larry didn't like a particular script, his answer was to throw up all over the set. Nerves? Method acting? I didn't stick around long enough to find out, but took refuge in the sanctuary of my dressing room instead.

In many ways, Larry was like a very talented, troubled child whose tantrums sometimes got the better of his self-control. The crew, however, quickly lost patience with him and vented their frustration by cutting him dead as often as possible and tormenting him however and whenever they could. Once when Larry demanded a cup of tea (as opposed to his habitual champagne), the crew, exasperated by his high-handedness and demands that a scene be reshot because he didn't like that particular segment of the script, put salt in his tea instead of sugar.

When the unsuspecting Larry took a sip and spat the tea out in disgust, the entire set rocked with suppressed laughter from the delighted crew, who probably would have applauded if they could have, they so enjoyed humiliating poor Larry.

But when it came to Gene Nelson, to whom Larry had taken an instant dislike when we shot the pilot, Larry hit out hard and often. And as much as I tried to avoid becoming involved in their clash, it was patently obvious that there was a lot of nastiness flying back and forth between the two of them during the early days of filming *I Dream of Jeannie*.

I was very secure in what I was doing in terms of my portrayal of Jeannie, and whenever a battle between Larry and Gene appeared to be on the horizon, I just hid away in my dressing room, as this was the only way I could survive the storms and conflicts that regularly raged on set. In fact, I retreated into my dressing room so often that many times I honestly didn't know what was brewing on the set.

Pretty soon, though, I made the unpleasant discovery that I was no longer able to remain above the fray. Larry's machinations created a situation that made it impossible for me to continue trying to rise above anything to do with *I Dream of Jeannie.*

After the first few episodes were aired on national TV, Larry demanded an audience with Sidney Sheldon, during which he complained, "Barbara is so little and so cute, and people keep coming up to me and asking how come I get so angry with this cute little thing. I look like I'm the bad guy, and I didn't sign on for that!"

When you consider Larry's iconic portrayal of J. R. Ewing, one of TV's all-time most memorable villains, his objections to being portrayed as the bad guy in *I Dream of Jeannie* now seem rather laughable. At the time, however, the issue was very important to him. So Sidney Sheldon called me into his office.

"Barbara, I've decided to change Jeannie's character a bit, and have her take charge more. I want you to be stronger," he announced.

"Stronger?" I said.

"Be stronger, Barbara, be stronger," Sidney replied.

Well, I'm an actress, and I believe I can play the strong woman (on- and offstage, as it happens) as well as any other actress in the business. No problem whatsoever. So, at Sidney's behest, strong I became, and I made a concerted effort to make Jeannie far more acerbic and willful than in the pilot and the few other episodes already aired.

When my two "strong" *I Dream of Jeannie* episodes were tested in front of a focus group, to my amusement word quickly came back to the producers that not one member of the focus group liked the new, stronger Jeannie. As a result, Sidney threw up his hands and told me to go back to playing Jeannie the way I'd played her in the first place!

As for the two "strong" episodes we'd already made, because I

*

was on maternity leave at the time, a much sweeter (in my opinion much too sweet) voice was dubbed over mine, and Jeannie was restored to her original persona.

Nonetheless, there were more clashes to come. Gene Nelson was a good friend of mine, and I liked and respected Larry as an actor, though his shifting moods and off-camera theatrics (arriving for work in a gorilla suit, for one) grew wearying. But it was clear that a showdown between Gene and Larry was imminent.

Unbeknownst to me, Larry decided to precipitate that showdown by issuing an ultimatum to Sidney: "Either Gene goes or I do."

Sidney, an intensely clever man, prevaricated. Then, without putting it in so many words, he threw down the gauntlet at my feet.

He invited me into his office and, after telling me that Jorja (his wife) sent her best and asking after my family, he got to the point. "Barbara, how would you feel if we replaced Larry?"

Now, I had no idea what was going on behind the scenes, but I did know one thing: no matter how anarchic Larry might be or how much the crew might detest him, when that camera rolled, he was *there*. He didn't have to be my best pal, just a good actor. And he definitely was that.

So I answered Sidney's question the only way I could. "Sidney, I feel it would be a big mistake to replace Larry. He really does his job, once the camera is rolling."

Before I knew it, Gene Nelson was out the door, without further ado. In all, he directed just eight episodes of *I Dream of Jeannie*. It must, however, be said that during the short period in which he directed the show, he stamped his indelible imprint on it. His contribution should never be underestimated, and I said as much at the time. But nothing could salvage my relationship with him. He never forgave me for siding with Larry, which was how he saw it, and he never talked to me again. Larry had gotten what he wanted.

*

One of the results of Larry's power play with Sidney was that he followed Sidney's advice to try to calm down while shooting *I Dream of Jeannie*. To that end, Sidney arranged for Larry to see a therapist, and, reluctantly or not, Larry went along with the idea. However, in keeping with the anything-goes ethos of the early sixties, the therapist ostensibly advised Larry to smoke pot and drink champagne on the set, to help himself relax.

Larry, being Larry, naturally didn't do anything by half measures. Henceforth, instead of being nervous, on edge, and confrontational, he started every day at the studio by drinking vast quantities of champagne, and in between scenes, he sequestered himself in his dressing room, smoking pot and downing yet more champagne, all in the interests of attaining a state of calm serenity. The result? Mayhem, as I'll tell you.

Surprisingly, the past master at handling Larry at his worst turned out to be Jackie Cooper, the former child star. Jackie was no longer an actor and had now graduated to the position of vice president of Screen Gems, the production company responsible for *I Dream of Jeannie*. Whenever Larry reverted to his usual modus operandi of questioning everything and everyone, as in "Do we *have* to do this? Do we *have* to do that?" Jackie would shoot back, "Do we *have* to pay you, Larry?" and despite himself, Larry couldn't prevent himself from laughing.

Larry even continued laughing when we had Groucho Marx, our first male guest star on *I Dream of Jeannie* (but I pity those that followed). Groucho, a close friend of Sidney Sheldon's, made a cameo appearance on the show in season two, in "The Greatest Invention in the World." Really, the most remarkable thing about Groucho's appearance on the show (which was extremely brief) was the fact that he waived his considerable fee—not out of friendship for Sidney, but simply because he didn't want to be liable for taxes.

*

Instead, he requested that he be compensated for his appearance on the show by being given a new TV set. He was.

Although I didn't remind Groucho of it at the time, I'd worked with him on his own show, years before, when I was Barbara Huffman and living at the Studio Club. I hadn't had any lines in the show, as I was basically just one of the dumb blond models he tended to hire and put in the background of the show. I was very young at the time, and my clearest memory of my walk-on in Groucho's show is that I was wearing a big gold ring on my left ring finger.

He took one look at it, wiggled his big cigar at me, and said, "Oh, so you're married, eh?"

I wasn't at the time, so I shook my head decisively.

Groucho wiggled his cigar at me again.

"Well, Miss Huffman, you're definitely sending a wrong message with that ring, then," he said with a wink.

Fortunately, Groucho's appearance on *I Dream of Jeannie* didn't upset the apple cart as far as Larry was concerned. Larry didn't have any problems working with Groucho, perhaps because Groucho was eighty years old and Larry didn't see him as competition.

Generally, though, people on the set felt that in Larry's mind, when it came to *I Dream of Jeannie,* he was the cock of the walk, and he definitely didn't want another rooster on his territory. He wanted to be the only leading man on the set, and to trumpet that the *I Dream of Jeannie* set was his domain and only his.

So it figured that when Sammy Davis Jr. guested on "The Greatest Entertainer in the World" in season two, it brought out the very worst in Larry. Having a star of Sammy's magnitude on *I Dream of Jeannie* would automatically upstage him.

When Sammy arrived on the set for the first time, intensely professional, friendly, and cheerful, I knew better than to mention the fact that I'd been in the chorus at Ciro's and that he'd sent an emissary to invite me out on a date.

Sammy was bright and funny, and we laughed a lot together. When I alluded to the news that although some black-and-white photos had been taken of us, they were now going to shoot some more, this time in color, he joked, "So now you're starting with all that racial stuff."

So far, so good. But when Larry strolled onto the set, you could immediately tell that Sammy was in for big trouble. Larry started by ordering Sammy around and telling him where to stand. Sammy, his own man in every sense of the term, was far from amused by Larry's overbearing manner.

It came time to shoot Sammy's most important scene, which required Larry to feed him his lines from off camera. As Sammy started saying his lines, Larry expressed his feelings about him in no uncertain terms by opening his mouth and letting loose a long, thick string of drool. I was in the scene and, against my will, couldn't help being mesmerized by the sight. Sammy, however, took it as a personal insult, which, of course, it was intended to be.

Quite understandably, he was incandescent with rage. He slammed off the set and shouted, "If I ever have to see that —— again, I'll kill him." Sammy was a big star, probably the biggest star who would ever guest on *I Dream of Jeannie,* and after a hurried, whispered conference, the director, Claudio Guzman, hustled Larry off the set and had someone other than Larry read Sammy his lines.

Afterward, Sammy took me aside and asked, "How in the hell do you work with this guy, Barbara? He's a total asshole."

Sammy's words, not mine.

Legendary comedian Milton Berle was one of the *I Dream of Jeannie* guest artists in Hawaii, where we shot "The Second Greatest

Con Artist in the World" for season three. By now, Larry was well established in the series and popular with the public, and so he felt safe flexing his muscles even further, flatly refusing to appear in the show with Milton. Which was probably just as well, because had Larry provoked him, Milton might well have resorted to his favorite party trick, exposing himself. His, um, endowment was rumored to be impressive, but I can't confirm that from personal experience. However, I do remember being unnerved when I caught sight of his bare feet. (And not because of the size!)

In the tropical Hawaii heat, most of us went barefoot whenever possible, but when Milton did, I couldn't help noticing that all his toes were crunched up. I didn't say a word, but he caught my expression and volunteered, "I was the last of six kids, Barbara, so I always got the smallest pair of shoes."

I wasn't quite sure that I had completely grasped the logic of that remark. But from then on, I understood why, during the shoot, Milton kept changing from one elegant, expensive pair of shoes to another pair that was even more elegant and expensive. As they say, you can take the star out of poverty, but you can never take poverty out of the star.

Nor can you take the bluntness out of someone who is congenitally blunt. At that time, Larry was probably the least diplomatic actor on the planet and would openly tell Sidney how much he hated his scripts.

Looking back, I don't think Sidney could have written *I Dream of Jeannie* any other way. The show was fantasy, light and fun entertainment—we weren't intending to be didactic in any way or Shakespearean in either language or scope.

Larry, however, was aiming higher and wasn't going to be satisfied by the perfectly serviceable scripts Sidney continued to churn out. Consequently, he let out his ire not just on celebrities but also on harmless "civilians" visiting the *I Dream of Jeannie* set. I've recounted the story about the nuns, so it followed that when I took the risk of inviting my mother to visit me on the set, I was terrified at the thought of what Larry might pull while she was there. At first he was at his most charming (and Larry is quite a charmer when he chooses to be). Then, all of a sudden, he cut her dead, and didn't speak to her again the entire day.

Hayden Rorke, who played Dr. Alfred Bellows in the series, was the one person involved with *I Dream of Jeannie* other than Jackie Cooper who could actually handle Larry. Our resident on-set terror, it transpired, actually respected Hayden in his own right, partly because Hayden was a friend of his mother, Mary Martin. Hayden even went so far as to tear into Larry for not bothering to read his script until the eleventh hour. Larry wouldn't have accepted that kind of a reprimand from anyone else, certainly not me. But he took Hayden's rebuke without complaining, because he respected him to such a high degree.

A native of Brooklyn, New York, Hayden came from a distinguished theatrical family. His grandfather was the well-known producer William Richardson Hayden, and his mother was an actress who later switched careers and built a business in textiles, after which she had the distinction of designing the material used in the ball gowns both Eleanor Roosevelt and Mamie Eisenhower wore at their respective husbands' inaugurations.

Hayden's impeccable acting credentials started out with his training at the American Academy of Dramatic Arts; he then appeared in classics with Walter Hampden's repertory company. During World War II, in which he was a sergeant, he toured with *This Is the Army,* and met Gene Nelson, who was also affiliated with the War Department.

After the war, Hayden became a successful professional actor, appearing in the Broadway productions of *The Philadelphia Story*, *The Country Wife*, *Three Men on a Horse*, *A Moon for the Misbegotten*, and *Dream Girl*. Moving on to Hollywood, he won fame as a character actor in such classic movies as *An American in Paris*. *The Unsinkable Molly Brown*, and *Pillow Talk*. His acting ability was superlative, and his grasp of the business served as an inspiration to all of us.

In his private life, Hayden was unashamedly gay. He and his partner, Justus Addiss, lived together for many years in Studio City, along with their menagerie of dogs. Hayden was wonderful in the part of Dr. Bellows, the psychiatrist forever stumped by Tony. Throughout the series, he remained a good friend to all of us and kept all our spirits up under all sorts of difficult circumstances, most of them caused by Larry. He was a prince, and everyone, even Larry, knew it.

Hayden's on-screen wife, Amanda Bellows, was played by the beautiful and gracious Emmaline Henry, whose Philadelphia pedigree melded with her visual resemblance to Grace Kelly. Initially a singer, with a rich soprano voice, Emmaline started out in radio, then moved to Hollywood and appeared in stage musicals, including the road company of *Gentlemen Prefer Blondes,* in which she took over from none other than Carol Channing, the star who'd attended Miss Holloway's school and inspired me to go there in the first place.

A well-known and glamorous fixture on TV shows such as *The Farmer's Daughter* and *Green Acres,* Emmaline also appeared in a slew of prestigious movies, including *Rosemary's Baby* and *Divorce, Italian Style.* Late in life, she fell in love and hoped to get married, but the man in question ultimately ditched her, and she was devastated, a fact that I firmly believe contributed to her death from cancer at the age of just forty-nine.

Before that, she appeared in thirty-nine episodes of *I Dream of*

Jeannie, starting in the second season (although she made a brief appearance during the first season as a magician's assistant whom Roger assumed was Jeannie's cousin). Her cool elegance attracted a great many fans and even fooled the censors into allowing her to show her navel during the beach scene in "Jeannie Goes to Honolulu." I, on the other hand, was encased in my red one-piece bathing suit and towels and forced to swelter away on Waikiki Beach. But I didn't begrudge Emmaline that freedom; she was a lovely, friendly lady and I liked her very much.

Barton MacLane, who played the imposing, if a little intimidating, General Peterson, started out in the 1920s as a Paramount contract player and was a veteran of over two hundred movies. In the legendary Bogart picture *The Maltese Falcon,* he played the police detective; he also appeared in Bogart's classic *The Treasure of the Sierra Madre* and in *Dr. Jekyll and Mr. Hyde.* An unusual man, passionate about card playing (he even invented a canasta card holder), he was in his late sixties when he made *I Dream of Jeannie,* and died during the making of the series.

Vinton Hayworth, who played General Schaeffer, only came into *I Dream of Jeannie* for the last two seasons. Nevertheless, he was a good actor; coincidentally, he was also Rita Hayworth's uncle. With his deep and resonant voice, he was a well-known radio announcer in his day, and also made countless guest appearances in shows other than *I Dream of Jeannie,* including *Perry Mason, The Beverly Hillbillies, The Munsters,* and *Gunsmoke.*

Bill Daily was fun and funny in real life, as well as in his role of Roger Healey in *I Dream of Jeannie.* Born in Des Moines, Iowa, he grew up in Chicago and, like Larry, began his career in the military (though as a musician, not as an actor). After performing in nightclubs in the Chicago area, he got a spot performing comedy routines on TV.

Discovered by Steve Allen, he went on to land guest roles in *Bewitched* and *The Farmer's Daughter.* Initially his role as Roger Healey on *I Dream of Jeannie* was projected to be a small one. But after Bill's natural comic talent shone through, his part was expanded, and the multidimensional Major Roger Healey came into being.

All of us on *I Dream of Jeannie* welcomed any laughs we could drum up amid the grueling shooting schedule. And now and again we enjoyed excursions the cast and crew took in the name of PR. We went to visit Cape Canaveral after Buzz Aldrin's rocket mission was scrubbed. I was photographed with Buzz, and then afterward all of the *I Dream of Jeannie* cast went on to Houston, where we saw the astronauts training to walk in outer space in a huge water tank. It was the nearest thing to being weightless on planet Earth. We were categorically warned to stay on the boardwalk overlooking the astronauts, no matter what.

"You do not get off the boardwalk, you do not go down below, you do not touch anything"—that was the rule.

We all obeyed, even Larry.

In another part of the facility, Gene Cernan was training in the moon module. Suddenly the distinguished astronaut shouted up at me, "Barbara, Barbara, come on down and see a mock-up of the capsule that's gonna land on the moon. Soon."

I hesitated.

"I can't, Gene," I said. "That's strictly against the rules."

A guard with us shook his head. "If Gene Cernan says you can go down, you can."

So I went down and got into the capsule, and he said, "Here, Barbara, you take the controls and land." I tried, but we "crashed." I was vastly relieved that it wasn't the real thing, but flying it was sure fun!

Given that Major Tony Nelson was an astronaut and, comedy

or not, the show did keep the image of the astronauts and the space program at the forefront of the public's consciousness, our links with NASA were strong. In June 1969, Cocoa Beach, Florida, celebrated Barbara Eden Day. All the local press and some national newspaper reporters and photographers were on hand.

Buzz Aldrin, who had guested on *I Dream of Jeannie,* showed up, and the photographers kept egging me on to kiss him. I planted a big kiss on his cheek, but that wasn't enough for the press, and not for Buzz, either. He grabbed me, declared, "I can do better than that," and kissed me right on the mouth. I wasn't prepared for that and was stunned, but everyone watching gave a big cheer.

A former fighter pilot and the first man to break the sound barrier, Chuck Yeager was also in an episode of *I Dream of Jeannie* ("Bigger than a Bread Box and Better than a Genie"), but for some obscure reason, his appearance in the show was not credited.

Such was Larry's respect for astronauts that he didn't act up during either Buzz's or Chuck's guest spot. He was also quietly respectful to Don Rickles, who guested on the episode "My Master, the Weakling," and who was wonderful. (A brief aside: the twenty-three-year-old David Soul, later of *Starsky and Hutch* fame, had a small part as an orderly in this episode as well.)

By now, Larry and Bill had fallen into the habit of always coming up with tough physical stunts they could do on the show. For this particular episode, they decided to roll down a hill. Rickles just stood at the top of the hill, watching. "Yeah, yeah, guy, beat yourself up, break your legs, go ahead. The genie's standing up here laughing; it's her show!" he said.

I liked him a lot, and I also liked his wife, who was called Barbara as well.

One night Michael, Charles Bronson, and I went to see Don Rickles in Las Vegas. When we walked into the room, he looked out into the audience, spotted me with my hair in big curls, and yelled out, "So you're married to a little girl, Michael Ansara!" We all laughed. As the show progressed, Rickles was at his funniest and most vitriolic, and the insults got stronger and stronger. He insulted Michael, he insulted Charlie, and he took on a few other audience members, but he never insulted me. Afterward, when we went backstage, he took me aside and said, "Barbara, I'm so sorry; I can't insult you. I can't say 'Barbara' and insult you, because, you see, I love my wife." Don Rickles, a wonderful comedian, was sometimes vicious and sometimes hurtful, but underneath he was a true romantic with a heart of gold.

* * *

At the height of the success of *I Dream of Jeannie,* I was receiving bags and bags of fan mail from all over the world. The series was so popular that in 1966, a Jeannie doll was released by Libby. There was also a Madame Alexander Jeannie doll, a Jeannie baby doll, and a Jeannie Barbie.

On the subject of *I Dream of Jeannie* objects, the original Jeannie bottle was a Jim Beam liquor decanter created in 1964 to help promote sales around Christmastime, painted with a leaf design in gold. It was the first of many designs and bottles used on the series. Years after the series became a hit, fans created their own versions of Jeannie bottles, which have become collectors' items.

I still own the original Jeannie bottle from the second season, which I keep locked in a bank safe deposit box. Before I deposited it there, I discovered that my Jeannie bottle truly did have magical powers. Until then I'd been keeping it on display in my library. But when a major earthquake struck Los Angeles in 1994, the library was totally destroyed. When I inspected the debris, however, there, shining out from the rubble like a glittering beacon, was my Jeannie bottle, wedged on top of a gigantic pyramid of books, as if by magic.

Part of the magic of *I Dream of Jeannie*, I suspect, was the aura of mystery surrounding the show and the characters. Famously, I never was allowed to expose my belly button on the show. Throughout the series, I kept getting letters from fans asking me if I had one, and visitors on the set always asked me to show it to them. I'd joke, "A nickel a peek!" but I never ripped away the last of the seven veils and revealed it.

However, the day came when, during the fourth season of *I Dream of Jeannie*, George Schlatter, my clever friend who used to produce *Rowan and Martin's Laugh-In*, came up with the brilliant idea of unveiling my hitherto unexposed belly button on an episode of his blockbuster TV show.

George had designed a tiny proscenium stage that would fit over my stomach. The plan was that a big fanfare would sound, the curtain would open, and a huge klieg light would shine on my belly button at last.

I was content to go along with George's off-the-wall idea, but NBC went ballistic. When I asked the producers to explain what was wrong with me unveiling my belly button on *Rowan and Martin's Laugh-In*, they just stared into space and ignored me. I wouldn't have given the issue any thought, but ever since the series began, I'd been receiving stacks of mail from U.S. soldiers posted abroad, who wrote, "I am so looking forward to seeing your belly button." Now that the belly button unveiling was nigh, I didn't want to disappoint them.

Truthfully, I didn't really understand what the fuss was about, and I still don't. I mean, every time I raised my arms on the show, my navel popped out, but clearly, neither the viewers nor the censors had ever noticed.

Now, though, that clever George Schlatter had made an issue of baring my belly button on national TV, NBC's honchos sat up and swung into action. A meeting was called for the studio's top brass, who all sat around a vast conference table debating the wisdom of exposing my belly button to the TV audience. George was present at that meeting and afterward joked, "I've never seen so many suits sitting around the table discussing a belly button!"

The verdict? Blackout on my belly button. Herminio Traviesas, NBC director of standards and practices, ruled that I was banned from showing it on *Rowan and Martin's Laugh-In*. Extraordinary—no appeal, no reprieve, nothing. My belly button remained shrouded for many years to come.

Even when the show went on location to Hawaii, where we shot three episodes in the sweltering heat, all the girls on Waikiki Beach wore bikinis, but I was asked to wear a chaste one-piece. At the time I thought the scenario was hilarious, but I didn't have a choice in the matter, so I made the best of it.

Making the best of it became my credo after Larry and I first heard that Jeannie and Tony were due to be married in the series. We were united in our reaction—sheer disgust—because we both knew that the wedding heralded the end of the show. After all, *I Dream of Jeannie*'s abiding theme was Jeannie's unrequited love for Major Nelson, his belief that she was just a figment of his imagination, and her stubborn insistence that she was real. Marrying her to Major Nelson derailed the plot and the series as a whole, and both Larry and I knew it.

However, filming the wedding proved to be fun. We shot it at Cape Canaveral (now the Kennedy Space Center), and when the episode was aired, it got one of the highest ratings of the entire series. But the writing was on the wall.

I wasn't particularly worried about the financial repercussions for my career if the show was canceled. During the third year of the show the producers had bought me out for a substantial sum, and although the show is still shown throughout the world today, I don't earn any residuals from it. However, I don't mind and never have. I was well paid.

After the wedding episode, we filmed fifteen more episodes, but we knew that it was just a matter of time before the show shuddered to a halt. Today we would say that when Jeannie and Tony got married, the show "jumped the shark." Larry, perhaps more than me, anticipated the impending demise of *I Dream of Jeannie* with a great deal of trepidation.

The fallout from Larry's misgivings about the show being on its last legs was—as Bill Daily was once quoted as saying—that he now spent most of his time hiding in his trailer. He flatly refused to talk to me or to anyone else. Not the most congenial way in which to co-star in a comedy series.

When I received the news from an agent that the show had been canceled (he baldly announced, "They didn't pick *I Dream of Jeannie* up again"), I felt just as if I had lost my family, albeit one with a wild, delinquent terror of a brother.

I adored being Jeannie. She was a part of my life for five years. Making *I Dream of Jeannie* was one of the most joyful experiences of my life. I loved playing Jeannie, and still think back on her with great affection, but I look at her as separate from me. She's not me. She's Jeannie.

chapter 9

VIVA LAS VEGAS

* * * * * * * * * * * * * * *

EVEN WHEN I was filming *I Dream of Jeannie*, I had always worked in my Las Vegas nightclub act and taken other roles on television and in movies. After the show was canceled, I just carried on working wherever and whenever I could.

And wouldn't you know it—my first post–*I Dream of Jeannie* job was with Larry! *A Howling in the Woods* was the uninspiring story of a justifiably jumpy wife who kept hearing (no prizes for guessing) a howling in the woods. In a piece of less-than-imaginative casting, none other than Larry Hagman played my husband.

My strongest memory of *A Howling in the Woods* was shooting by the shores of Lake Tahoe and being asked by the director to film a scene in a little boat on the lake. The director and the cinematographer were in the boat with Larry and me, as they needed some close-up shots of the two of us on the lake together.

All of a sudden, right in the middle of the lake, the boat's engine started sputtering, then cut out completely. To our dismay, we discovered that we only had one oar with us in the boat. What had happened to the other one, no one knew.

So there we were, marooned in a tiny boat on Lake Tahoe. We quickly agreed that our only option was to sit back and wait to be rescued. We knew that when the rest of the crew realized how long we'd been away from shore, they'd come looking for us.

However, *when* that might happen was anybody's guess. Moreover, it was lunchtime, we were all starving, and the only thing we had to eat between us was a little packet of M&M's that I had in my pocket. To our relief, we were rescued after one and a half hours.

Larry and I had a certain amount of camaraderie while making *A Howling in the Woods* together. But it was a strange feeling not to have my *I Dream of Jeannie* family around me anymore. I wasn't happy that the show had ended, but I wasn't depressed. That came later.

Instead, I threw myself into my Las Vegas nightclub act with a vengeance. The idea of returning to my singing roots and appearing in my very own Vegas act had taken root while I was still appearing in *I Dream of Jeannie* and wanted to work during the hiatus between seasons.

My new career kicked off after two young men who'd made a hit record with Shelley Fabares got in touch with me and asked if they could do a demo with me. Well, I've never been one to back down from a career challenge, so I agreed, and we cut an album and then took it to my agent, Shep Fields.

Unfortunately, Shep rejected the boys and the demo album out of hand, but the idea of a solo Las Vegas act clearly stayed with him. And in 1967 Shep secured a contract for me.

At first I was confident and not the least bit nervous about taking on Las Vegas. A writer and a musician were hired to create the act. When we rehearsed the show, I felt good about it, and my prospects of success seemed high.

It was only two days before the show was due to open at the Shamrock Hotel in Houston (kind of a dress rehearsal for the Frontier Hotel in Las Vegas) that it finally dawned on me how truly terrible it really was. It might have been perfect as a high school production, but it wasn't what I believed a large-scale Vegas production ought to be.

Let me give you a flavor of the fiasco that my first Las Vegas show seriously was. The curtain opens, and there onstage is a larger-than-life replica of my Jeannie bottle. Meanwhile, I'm out of the view of the audience, scurrying up a ladder and into my bottle, where I am supposed to sit and sing my first song.

This is what those writers came up with (more or less): "Sitting in my bottle, on my Persian rug / Thinking of Aristotle, and drinking from a jug." Then the script had me morph into an embryo, curl up, and sing something along the lines of, "Today I will open my eyes! Blink! Today I'll be moving my fingers! Blink! Today I'll be taking my first steps! Blink! Today I'm alive!"

An embryo, in Las Vegas. Gee whiz!

The show went on and on in the same vein, culminating with me standing onstage wearing a gray wig and belting out a song in my guise of an old lady. Entertainment? I don't think so.

At the eleventh hour, in desperation, I contacted veteran choreographer Nick Castle (who had choreographed Betty Grable, Ann Miller, Gene Kelly, and Fred Astaire and staged countless TV and Las Vegas shows) and begged him fly to Las Vegas to fix mine. When he arrived, I showed him what we had, eager to find out what he thought of the show and what he felt he could do to salvage it.

After a few minutes in which Nick seemed lost in thought, he pronounced his final verdict on my first Las Vegas show.

"Can't fix it. Throw it out, Barbara. Just stand onstage and sing," he declared.

Unfortunately, the show had to go on, just as it was, until the end of the run. But the following year I put Nick's suggestions into practice: I stood on the stage and sang, and I danced a little. My new Las Vegas nightclub act was given a tryout at the College Inn, Chicago, in August 1969. When the audiences didn't throw rotten tomatoes at me, I gave a massive sigh of relief, then took my act to the Frontier Hotel in Las Vegas.

Like many other female entertainers who worked Las Vegas, I hired the incredibly gifted Bob Mackie to design my gowns for the show. Renowned as the "Sultan of Sequins" and the "Rajah of Rhinestones," Bob had won seven Emmys and designed gowns for Diana Ross, Liza Minnelli, Raquel Welch, Cher, Barbra Streisand, and, interestingly enough, Lucille Ball (who, judging by how beautifully she embellished my gown for the "Country Club Dance" episode of her show, was clearly fond of a rhinestone or two herself). Most of all, Bob was celebrated for his long-term association with Carol Burnett, for whom he made the most fabulous gowns.

When it came to designing the wardrobe for my nightclub act, in a quest to make me look as glamorous as possible, Bob placed beads strategically all over my gowns. However, the gowns were so skintight that wearing underwear was totally out of the question. As a result, when the light struck me a certain way, the orchestra members could see my body in every intimate detail. They were unperturbed: this was Las Vegas and they were 100 percent unshockable.

My mother, however, proved to be quite a different story. A few years ago, I ran into Tony Orlando, who had headlined at the MGM Grand in Las Vegas at the same time as I did. "Your mother was very protective of you," he began.

"Not particularly," I said, slightly surprised, but pleased that he'd mentioned my mother, who had passed on twenty years before.

Tony laughed.

"You don't know the half of it," he said. "Every night, when you were singing, I stood in the wings to watch you. But then your mother would notice and glare at me. 'You can't stay here. Not with Barbara wearing *that*!' she said, and shooed me away from the wings."

I looked up to the sky for a second and said a quick but heartfelt thanks to her.

Which reminds me of the time in 1973 when Gene Schwam, my manager to this day, called me out of the blue and asked me point-blank: "Barbara, are you interested in making a million dollars?"

Well, of course I was, I told him.

There was a long pause at the other end of the line.

"Brace yourself, Barbara," Gene said. "It involves nudity!"

"How much?" I asked, hoping against hope that he would say a glimpse of cleavage or maybe a peek at my navel.

No such luck. It turned out that *Playboy* had offered a million dollars for me to pose nude in the magazine.

Barbara Jean Huffman, a *Playboy* centerfold?

I didn't have to think twice about my answer!

* * *

My first Vegas act at the Frontier opened with a line of chorus girls, not that far removed in spirit from the Ciro's chorus line all those years ago. And in the line was a bubbly blond dancer with a giggle that would one day launch a thousand jokes. Just before my entrance, she and I would chat in the wings. Even then, Goldie Hawn knew exactly what she wanted and where she was heading in terms of her career. I remember her proudly telling me that she was going to Hollywood and that a very important person was going to help her. I never discovered his name, but he was clearly true to his word.

During that first season in Las Vegas, I made a number of unpleasant discoveries. First, just as Elvis had confided to me all those years ago on the set of *Flaming Star*, any singer worth his or her salt playing Las Vegas had to stay in the hotel room most of the time. Despite all the superficial glamour and glitter on offer in the entertainment capital of the world, playing there was very uncomfortable for me because of the loneliness—the same loneliness Elvis had suffered from. It was uncomfortable for another reason, too—the dry Las Vegas air played havoc with the vocal cords.

Performing live had some downsides I'd never expected. On one dreadful occasion, performing at a hotel in Arizona, I received a threatening letter telling me that if I didn't stand outside a particular church in town at a particular time, I would die. Initially I tried to ignore the letter and even was stupid enough to try to tell myself to "rise above it." But then my common sense took over and I told my manager about the letter. He called the police, and in a flash guards were posted outside my dressing room and my hotel room, and bodyguards followed me wherever I went, day and night, which was a great relief. But the police still viewed the death threat against me with extreme seriousness. So at the appointed time, a policewoman who bore a strong resemblance to me was sent to stand outside the church. Thank the Lord, the stalker never materialized and I never heard from him again.

Another time, I was in Switzerland on a PR trip with my close friend Dolores Goldstein, whose son went to school with my son, Matthew. While we were there, Dolores, who was screening my phone calls, took what seemed like a harmless call from a young man who seemed to know various people who worked for me (including my manager and some of his office employees). He said that he had just graduated from college with honors, and would I be so kind as to autograph a picture of myself for him and mail it to him?

It was a sweet, innocent request. At the time I thought nothing of it, and so I wrote on the photo, "I am so happy you did so well at college. You deserve it."

A few weeks later, Dolores got a call at the Showboat, in Atlantic City, where I was doing my act, asking if she knew the young man who had asked for the picture. To her consternation, Dolores was told that he was at the hotel and had insisted not only that he knew me but also that he knew many people who worked or traveled with me, including her.

According to the police, he kept demanding to see me. He was behaving extremely suspiciously and insisting that I knew him. As proof, he handed the police the picture I had signed. Much later, it finally dawned on me that the autograph did give the impression that we knew each other well. I'd been set up.

At the time, though, Dolores didn't want to frighten me, so she said nothing to me about the young man. Instead, she assured the police that neither she nor I nor anyone else in my employ knew him. She was shocked when the police asked her to go downstairs, where the young man was in custody, and walk past him. Their argument was that if his face lit up with recognition when he saw her, his story would be proved true. But if he gave no sign whatsoever of knowing Dolores, the police would know that he was as suspect as she had said he was.

With a great many misgivings, and without telling me, Dolores walked past the young man. Seeing her, he didn't give even a flicker of recognition. So the police threw him out of the hotel, and Dolores, believing that the situation had been defused, didn't tell me that anything had happened.

However, a couple of days later, she and I were having dinner in the hotel restaurant when she received a call from the police warning us that the young man had somehow eluded security and snuck back into the hotel. At that point, Dolores came clean and told me the truth. The police promptly whisked us out the back door of the restaurant and up into my suite. From then on, I had twenty-four-hour security and was glad of it.

Performing in front of a live audience can have its fair share of surprises.

I played on the same bill as the brilliant comedian Shecky Greene for three years at the MGM Grand. One evening my act seemed to go exceptionally well, and the audience gave me a rousing ovation. Afterward, feeling tired but happy, I stayed in the wings to watch Shecky's hilarious routine, the way I always did.

Shecky was always upbeat and genial after he finished his act. But that night when he took his bows and then walked offstage, I could sense that something was seriously wrong.

"How in the hell can they expect me to make an audience laugh when they've got a dead guy in the audience right in front of me?" he growled.

"A dead guy?" I said, my eyes practically popping out of my head.

Shecky walked back onstage again to take a final bow, so he couldn't immediately answer my question.

When he came offstage again to the sound of uproarious applause, he didn't keep me in suspense for long.

"Well, Barbara, I'm trying to make jokes and there's a dead guy out front," he said.

At first I thought he was trying out a black humor comedy routine on me, but I didn't laugh.

Nor did Shecky. He went on, "A guy in the front row had a heart attack, so they hustled his wife out of the room and put a tablecloth over the guy and left him there."

I thought back to my last song. Of course! Although the

spotlights had been shining straight into my eyes, I remembered noticing a big expanse of white cloth in the first few rows, though I hadn't been able to make out what it was.

"He had the heart attack while you were singing," Shecky explained helpfully. But at least he had the good grace not to make a crack about "killing him softly with your song" or "knocking them dead."

Working in front of humans is one thing; working in the same show as an elephant is quite another. When I played the Nugget in Reno in 1986, I sang songs like "I Go to Rio," "I Will Survive," and "I Can't Smile Without You," and the twice-nightly shows were opened by Bertha, the Nugget's very own performing elephant.

My contract at the Nugget stipulated that I had to do two shows a night, seven nights a week, but lucky Bertha got one day a week off, so that she could enjoy a day of first-class grooming, with massages and manicures. I was almost jealous.

Seriously, though, I've always loved elephants. They're such darlings, intelligent and very family oriented. So for many years I have collected elephant ornaments wherever and whenever I happen to find them.

Since my time working with Simm, the African lion on *I Dream of Jeannie* (and as a Leo myself), I've always adored lions as well. And it wasn't a coincidence that when I made my 1972 special, *Love Is . . . Barbara Eden,* we had a young male lion in the act with me. The idea was that the lion would be onstage with me, standing in the middle of a Mylar circle and looking kingly.

However, when his trainer led the lion over to the Mylar, the poor lion assumed that it was water, tentatively tried to stick his paw in it, then shook the paw as if it had gotten wet. Undeterred, I started singing "The Look of Love" to him (why in heaven's name the script called for me to do that, who knows), and he promptly lay down on the floor and fell fast asleep. So we did another take. This time I was fortunate that he didn't fall asleep. Instead, he started chewing my chair and really enjoying the taste of it. He chewed away, happy and content, until an exasperated Gene hollered down from the rafters, "Get rid of the lion!"

So much for my special touch with lions!

One of my favorite Las Vegas stars was George Burns. I first worked with him in June 1972 at the Frontier Hotel. He was a gentleman, and so much fun to be with.

When I arrived at the hotel, I discovered that George's dressing room was a large house trailer with two bedrooms, a living room, and a kitchen, while mine was just a very small room. That was fine by me, but when George found out, he was livid and said, "Why are you stuck in that little room down there, Barbara? Let's share my trailer!"

George was seventy-three years old at the time, and I moved into his trailer and used it as my dressing room without giving a single thought to my reputation. During the run, George's friends Jack Benny and Edward G. Robinson often came to the dressing room to chew the fat with him. Most of the time I would just sit around listening to their funny stories and their perceptive critiques of George's act, and I enjoyed every minute of it.

The most fun thing about George, though, was that in between shows he'd announce, "Okay, Barbara, let's go get some soup!" Normally when I played Las Vegas I never left my dressing room between shows, because if I did, I was always stopped by autograph seekers. It's flattering, but not when you've got limited time and are headed out to a restaurant for dinner. But strolling through the casino with George was fine. He'd just amble through the crowds with me and say to all the fans who came up to him, "Hi, hi, sorry, no time now," and keep on walking till we reached the restaurant, where we'd sit down and have our soup. While we ate, a crowd usually gathered around us, but no one bothered us.

When George and I started working together, his beloved wife, Gracie Allen, had long since died, and he had his young girlfriend, a student at UCLA, with him. Every morning I'd look out of my hotel room window and see George swimming back and forth in the pool and this young girl sitting there doing her homework. Funnily enough, each time I worked with George in Las Vegas, he always had a different young girlfriend with him. Were the girls for real or just for show? I couldn't tell you. But he was a good guy, fun to be with and really nice to me.

Although he probably didn't realize it at the time, George turned out to be also a major influence on young Matthew's life. Years after George and I played Vegas together, when Matthew was a teenager, Michael and I had dinner with George in Las Vegas.

George asked, "So does the kid want to be an actor?"

"Very much," I said, and grimaced.

"Couldn't be better," George said adamantly.

Michael and I both shook our heads.

George raised an eyebrow. "But show business has been so good to you two," he said, wagging a finger at us disapprovingly.

After dinner, Michael and I had a long debate about Matthew and his future career. In the end, after much discussion, we ultimately concluded that we shouldn't stand in the way of Matthew becoming an actor after all.

And all because of George Burns.

In a way, you could say that he really did play God that night, because he certainly did create a new world for Matthew.

*   *   *

Las Vegas being Las Vegas, I also rubbed shoulders with other performers, many of them show business legends, among them Dean Martin and Jerry Lewis. Dean was fun, a lovely man, and I adored working with him. He never rehearsed, but no one really expected him to. Offstage he was exactly the same person you saw onstage or on TV—a cool guy with a little drink in his hand. A real one, of course.

When I was appearing in Lake Tahoe, Liza Minnelli, who was headlining at the hotel across the road, came to see my second show and visited me in my dressing room afterward. We sat on the floor and laughed like crazy and had a good time together. She was just darling. For a while I felt like we could become good friends. But in subsequent meetings I sensed that although she was always warm and friendly to me, she still kept a shield in front of her; it protects her, but no one can ever really crack it and get through to the real Liza behind it.

Along the way, I also often guested on other people's TV shows. When Gene Kelly was a guest on one of the TV shows I hosted, I found out at the last minute that I was scheduled to do a tap dance with him. That was terrifying in the extreme.

I was vastly relieved to find that Gene was a kind and patient teacher who was prepared to rehearse the number over and over with me. Afterward, I rehearsed for a few hours more on my own, just to make sure I got it right. In the end, I was fairly confident that I'd mastered the routine, and was even looking forward to doing it with Gene on the show.

Imagine my dismay, then, when at the final rehearsal he came over to me with a towel around his neck and said, "Hey, kid" (he called everyone he worked with "kid," no matter how young or old they were), "you know, I think I want to change something in the routine."

I visibly blanched, but I was much too in awe of Gene to protest. So we spent the next few hours learning the new steps, and then I put in a few more hours practicing them alone.

On the night of the show, I was step-perfect. Gene, however, was not. Afterward, he took me aside and with a twinkle in his eye said, "You know who the audience is going to think did the routine right, don't you?"

"I know, Gene," I said, throwing up my hands in despair. "You, of course."

And I was correct, because everyone I talked to who saw the show marveled at the perfection of Gene Kelly's dancing, whereas my efforts passed without comment.

Lee Marvin, famous for his rough, macho-man persona, guested with me on a TV special but turned out to be a pussycat. When he had to lift me during one of our routines, he kept asking, "Are you all right, Barbara? You're so little. Are you all right?" I assured him that I was.

Many years before meeting me, Michael dated Cher's mother, Georgia Holt, and when I was on Cher's show, she joked, "I used to sit on Michael's knee when I was little, Barbara."

I burst out laughing, but that wasn't unusual when Cher and I were together. She always made me laugh so much—we were like two schoolgirls together. I worked with Sonny Bono as well, but fun as that was, working with Cher, whether singing or in a skit, was always my preference. She's bright, sassy, and very grounded.

In March 1965 I was a guest on a show with Mickey Rooney, Dean Martin, and Kate Smith. Mickey is an incredible performer, really out there, but of course he's very small. Dean was medium height. Kate, in contrast, was really big, both in height and in width. At the end of the show, the four of us were slated to sing a medley of "Yankee Doodle Dandy" and "My Old Kentucky Home" together, all standing in a row; Kate, then Dean, then me, then Mickey. It crossed my mind that we looked like a flight of steep steps.

We started singing our song together. Then Mickey raised his hand and the band stopped playing. He took Kate aside and they started whispering together. Looking at them, I could guess what they were whispering about. The end result? I was placed in the middle, like strawberry jam in an oddly shaped sandwich.

For many years, one of my greatest joys was touring with Bob Hope—or rather, Mr. Hope, as I respectfully addressed him when we met in person. To me, Bob Hope was always the quintessential all-around entertainer and a great comedian. If you see some of his early movies, you know he was not merely a comedian but a good actor as well. He was smart, and a fabulous raconteur to boot.

Offstage, however, he was a bit of a rascal with women.

As I got to know Bob better, I discovered that he nurtured the archaic, chauvinistic conviction that all women were divided into two distinct categories: ladies and the other kind. And he had very firm ideas about exactly who was a lady and who was not.

Fortunately for me, he decided early on in our acquaintance that I belonged in the "lady" category. After that, he was very protective of me, primarily because he felt I merited it. So one time, when some football players were on Bob's show and became overly familiar with me, Bob took them aside and said sternly, "No, no, guys, she's not for you. Besides, there's a big Indian at home."

The guys backed off, and I was grateful. Bob himself always treated me with the greatest respect. I loved him and treated him with due respect in return. In that spirit, we toured the world together in 1988 on his USO-sponsored "Around the World in 8 Days" tour, and Bob was kind enough to allow Matthew to join us on it. Together with Bob, we circled the globe in eight days, traveled twenty-seven thousand miles, and in the process entertained twenty-five thousand servicemen stationed in the Persian Gulf. The tour took us from Honolulu to Clark Air Base in the Philippines, Diego Garcia in the Indian Ocean, the battleship USS *Iowa,* the USS *Okinawa,* and Bahrain.

Our first stop was the USS *Midway,* a nuclear aircraft carrier positioned at the mouth of the Persian Gulf. We spent one night aboard, and I remember being so happy that I was finally able to wash my hair.

Our final show was supposed to be at Lajes Field in the Azores, but winds of fifty-one knots kept our C-141 Starlifter transport from taking off. Bob, however, was unfazed and continued hitting golf balls off the deck of the *Okinawa.* Ultimately, we didn't make it to the Azores because of the weather, but helicoptered to Bahrain, where we spent several days. I remember a lovely party at the American embassy there; I thought I was back in Jeannie's home! From there we flew to Italy in C-130s, which normally carried troops and equipment—very basic and raw!

On plane trips between stops, the rest of us were usually asleep, exhausted, but Bob rarely slept and spent much of the journey cutting and splicing the day's TV tape. He was eighty-five at the time.

On average, we slept four hours a night, and the plane refueled in midair. One night I was sleeping the sleep of the dead when all of a sudden I woke up with a start: it was Bob, telling me that the plane was being refueled and that I ought to watch. I nodded and then fell straight back to sleep again. But you can bet your boots that Bob stayed awake all night and watched that plane being refueled.

On another tour, Connie Stevens was traveling with us on a C-130 cargo plane. Bob had the lower part of a bunk bed, because of his age, but Connie and I were supposed to sleep on the floor. Bob took pity on us and said that if we ever wanted to, we could take a nap in the top bunk. So one night, fed up with sleeping on the floor, Connie and I slept toe to head in the bunk above Bob's. Or at least we tried to—our sleep was hampered by the fear that the top bunk would break in the middle of the night, land on top of Bob, and crush him, which would lead to the headline "Two Blondes Kill Bob Hope!"

Aside from being part of Bob's USO tours, I regularly appeared on his TV specials (on the Christmas specials our tradition was always to sing "Silver Bells" together), sang with him to an audience of fifteen thousand in Chicago, and in 1968 I opened the new Madison Square Garden with him. On that momentous occasion, I made my entrance into the arena in a brown fur coat, carrying a big bunch of balloons, then removed the coat to reveal a ringmaster's costume underneath. From then on, I sang and danced in a series of outfits: an ice skater's costume (in which I danced to "The Skater's Waltz"), a cowboy getup, and a tennis dress. The whole sequence ended up with me dressed as Uncle Sam, all intensely patriotic and the epitome of good old-fashioned American values, everything for which Bob Hope so proudly stood. Later that same year Bob and I did a special together at NASA in Houston, at the end of which he brought all the astronauts onstage, which was great fun. And when Bob was seventy-five, we performed in Australia at the Perth Entertainment Centre in front of an audience eight thousand strong. Bob didn't work with anyone he didn't like, so I guess he liked me as much as I liked him.

Although Bob Hope was such a big star, he was a regular guy. I'll never forget the time in St. Louis when we were working at the Fox Theater and Bob suddenly said, "Let's go get an ice cream cone." So we just walked down the main street together, eating ice cream cones, and nobody bothered us. They had such respect for Bob, as I did.

We shared the same sense of humor, I think, and I always loved it when we did a comic duet of the song "Help Me Make It Through the Night." A little naughty and suggestive, but that was Bob, and when all was said and done, it was good, clean fun.

My relationship with singer Tom Jones, however, is quite another story. I worked with Tom in England in March 1969, during a break from *I Dream of Jeannie,* and flew to England with my manager, Gene Schwam, my conductor, Doug Talbert, and my hairdresser, Mary Skolnik, to guest on *This Is Tom Jones.* My guest spot consisted of me singing a duet with Tom, "The Look of Love," while we strolled along the Thames embankment together.

I've always known that my strength as a singer lies more in my acting ability than in my singing voice, so my method has always been to act my songs, very much the way that Rex Harrison did in the musical *My Fair Lady.* So when I sang "The Look of Love" to Tom, I sang the lyrics with warmth and passion, true to the sentiments behind the words. We strolled along the Thames embankment together and finished up at the top of a stone staircase in the moonlight. When the music stopped and the cameras were switched off, Tom took my hand, looked deep in my eyes, and said in his gravelly Welsh baritone, "Can I show you London, Barbara?"

My first reaction was that his request was a friendly offer made by a Brit to an American who'd never visited London before, and to whom he was gallantly volunteering to show the sights. But then he started caressing my hand sensually.

If I had any further doubts about Tom's intentions in offering to show me London, my manager immediately clarified the matter for me. "He thought you were coming on to him, because you put so much passion into the song. He really thought you meant every word of the lyrics you were singing to him," he whispered to me.

At that moment, the director called for Tom and me to do another take of the duet. This time I didn't inject an iota of passion, meaning, or intensity into my voice, but just sang the words in a monotone, almost by rote. The moment the director yelled, "Cut," Gene rushed over to me and said accusingly, "You've toned it down, Barbara. What's wrong with you?"

"But Gene, you're the one who warned me that Tom believed I meant what I was singing to him! And that gave him the wrong idea about how I felt about him, big-time!" I said indignantly.

"You can handle Tom Jones, Barbara. I know you can," he replied. "Give the song everything you've got."

So I did. I sang "The Look of Love" to Tom as if he were the love of my life, the man I desired more than any other man on the planet. And again Tom must have believed me, because the moment the camera was switched off, he put his arm around me and said, "Can I show you London, Barbara?"

I whispered back, "But Tom, I'm married!"

"Well, so am I!" Tom replied, quick as a flash.

We parted company and I had dinner all by myself in my hotel room, then went to bed.

At four in the morning, the phone suddenly ripped me out of my sleep. In a daze, I picked up the receiver, terrified that something might have happened to Matthew or to Michael.

But I needn't have worried.

"Barbara, can I show you London?" Tom said again in that sexy baritone.

"Tom! It's four in the morning!" I said.

Tom chuckled. "Don't you worry about the time, Barbara. I'll show you London right now!"

"Tom, we've got a show to do tomorrow! And it's *your* show!" I said, as if I were reprimanding a naughty boy, which, of course, he was at that moment.

In Michael's studio. Michael is a very talented artist, and these paintings of his mother, his sister, and his father are perfect examples of his work.

With Michael in the garden of our second home in Sherman Oaks. We were happily married and looking forward to the future with hope and optimism.

Michael and I are bliss-
fully happy with our
newborn son, Matthew.

I'm with
one-and-a-
half-year-old
Matthew,
who's holding
the phone.

Larry and I are with Simba, the lion, just before Simba gave a big roar. Larry and every other man on the set raced out of the studio in terror. Meanwhile, Simba put his head in my lap and purred!

Larry and I on the set of *I Dream of Jeannie*. Although we look serene and content here, when the camera was switched off, life was far from uneventful.

Groucho was a guest star on *I Dream of Jeannie*. This was our second meeting, but I decided not to mention our first to him.

A peaceful moment among Larry and Sammy Davis Jr. and me captured just before all hell broke out between Larry and Sammy off camera.

A publicity shot promoting my Las Vegas act, showcasing me in a Bob Mackie gown.

A still from the movie *Harper Valley PTA*, which was also Woody Harrelson's first feature film. Afterward, I went on to make the TV series of the same name.

Showing my belly button at last! A publicity shot from *I Dream of Jeannie: 15 Years Later.*

Harnessed, about to jump, and feeling petrified in a scene from *Your Mother Wears Combat Boots,* shot at Fort Benning, Georgia.

With my second husband, Chuck Fegert, at a publishing convention in Florida, where he was probably the life and soul of the entire event.

Mommy at my new house in Beverly Hills, which was in the process of being decorated. We thought it would be fun to pose for this picture sitting on the floor and enjoying it.

With Matthew at his cousin's wedding. This photograph touches my heart, as Matthew, in his rented tuxedo, had made such a great effort to be with me that day. I could tell that he wasn't well at all, but I was still glad he was there with me.

Such a contrast: Matthew in rehab, free and clear of drugs, looking bright and healthy, with all of life ahead of him. Or so it seemed to us both that day. Jon, who was with us, took this photograph.

With my current husband, Jon, at his company Christmas party, happy together then and forever.

He hung up the phone without another word.

About three hours later, I arrived at the studio and went straight into makeup. Tom was already there in the chair, having his make-up done.

"Good morning, Tom," I said, trying to act as if nothing had happened between us just hours before.

Tom turned away from me abruptly and didn't answer.

A few moments later the makeup artist left the room, and Tom finally looked me in the eye.

"Four in the morning, Tom?" I said.

"Oh, you were lucky, Barbara," he retorted. "I nearly knocked your door down."

I don't want to disillusion anyone, but the truth is that if Tom Jones had indeed knocked down my door, I might well have succumbed.

* * *

Generally, I was always delighted by the enthusiasm and loyalty of my audiences. When I played Hot Springs, Arkansas, there was a tremendous tornado; windows were torn out of shops and houses, and cars were upended, but we still had an enthusiastic audience at the show that night.

Other times, however, the audience's enthusiasm can be over-whelming, not to say a little scary. In the early seventies, I headlined at the Waldorf-Astoria for a convention of the heavy equipment contractors' union. I was to wear a sheer Bob Mackie gown covered in beads. Dinner was scheduled for six, and the show was supposed to begin at eight.

In the middle of the afternoon, I donned my Bob Mackie and got ready to go onstage to rehearse for an hour. To my extreme annoyance I was then informed that the stage hadn't yet been built. I tried to remain calm.

Almost beside himself with fury, my manager, Gene, shouted to someone to get the head union official immediately.

When the man appeared, tall and classically tough-looking, Gene flatly informed him, "Sorry, we can't rehearse because there's no stage. And if we can't rehearse, Miss Eden can't sing tonight."

The union official came right up to Gene and stuck his face close to his.

"Miss Eden had better sing tonight," he said, "or you better get a fast pair of roller skates."

Gene didn't hesitate. "Okay," he said.

Just before I was about to go onstage at eight, I got word there had been a further delay in building the stage. By ten in the evening, there was still no stage.

At eleven-thirty a union official came to get me, so I assumed the stage had been completed. But when I arrived in the packed ballroom, to my shock the stage still hadn't been built, and all the musicians were sitting ready in their chairs right in the middle of the floor.

So without any rehearsal, I faced an audience of a thousand union men, each and every one of them dressed in black tie and tails (I thought they looked like a bunch of penguins) and all hollering at the top of their voices, "Where's Jeannie, where's Jeannie?"

I started the show with a rousing, fast song, but then switched moods and sang a soft version of "MacArthur Park" and "Didn't We." Even so, all the way through the songs, the guys were yelling, "Hey, Barbara, where ya from?" and "Honey, sing 'Melancholy Baby,'" and, "Come on, Jeannie baby, flash us your navel!"

All of a sudden, as if someone had given them a secret signal, a big group of union guys surged toward me and started to sing "Sweet Georgia Brown," a completely different song from the one I was struggling to get through.

When someone turned the lights out, that did it—Gene and I sneaked out of the building as fast as we could, grabbed a cab, and hightailed it to La Guardia.

Touring brought with it other, less intimidating moments. Once I was appearing in concert in Detroit (in a theater the stage of which was built over an ice-skating rink), and my friend Mary shared a room with me. Just before we went to bed, I saw that she was readying herself to sleep stark naked.

As diplomatically as possible, I said, "But Mary, what if there's a fire in the middle of the night?"

"There won't be, Barbara, there won't be." She laughed, then turned over and went to sleep, naked as the day she was born.

The fire alarm rang out about an hour later.

I grabbed my show costumes, my makeup, and my music and made for the door. Mary, meanwhile, made a terrified dash for her clothes and threw them on as fast as she could. And, to my credit, I didn't even say *I told you so.* Together, we dashed out into the freezing streets, in the middle of a heavy snow.

One of the hotel maids kindly offered us the opportunity to sit in her car, and we gratefully accepted. A few minutes later, a fireman rapped on the car window, asking us if we'd left anything important in the hotel room. I thanked him and said that all we'd left behind was some nail polish.

Without a word, he walked away. Ten minutes later, he brought us down our bottles of nail polish, having risked his life to go back to the hotel room to get them. Mary and I were speechless.

Then we took one look at Gene, who'd come down in a red leather jacket and red shoes, and we both screamed, "Gene! You're dressed for a fire," and burst out laughing.

Sadly, the days of untrammelled fun and laughter were numbered.

chapter 10

TRAGEDY

* * * * * * * * * * * * * *

MICHAEL ANSARA TRULY was the love of my life, the passion of my youth, and the father of my only son. I adored being married to him. But by 1971, a year after the cancellation of *I Dream of Jeannie,* he had less and less work, money was scarcer, and tensions were escalating in our marriage.

When we first met, Michael had been the star, and I was just a struggling contract player in her first TV series. But when *I Dream of Jeannie* burst into our lives, the tables were turned. In a scenario that echoed *A Star Is Born,* writers, photographers, and fans didn't flock to Michael as they had when he was in *Broken Arrow* and a star; instead, they were almost exclusively centered on me.

Michael tried everything to revive his career, but after *Broken Arrow* was canceled, he was mostly cast as villains and heavies in movies, and was never the star. He suffered for not being a blue-eyed, blond-haired all-American boy. While I made sure to defer to him in most things, such as decorating the house and finances, and always encouraged him with his oil painting, at which he was extremely talented, there was no question that our marriage came under a strain because of my success in *I Dream of Jeannie.* Even when the series had ended and I was appearing in my Las Vegas nightclub act, the tensions between Michael and me continued to escalate.

That's not to say we didn't still have our happy times together. Michael was a great dirt bike enthusiast, and at the height of *I Dream of Jeannie,* we bought a Yamaha 360cc dirt bike for him and a 125cc Yamaha dirt bike for me. To my surprise, I got as much of a thrill out of dirt bike riding as he did, though I didn't have as much time as I'd have liked in which to practice.

However, I wasn't that comfortable about riding on the streets, which proved to be somewhat of a problem, as dirt bike areas are only accessible via the roads. Nonetheless, we circumvented the problem a few times by putting the bikes on the trailer, driving it to Palm Springs, and riding them there, which was glorious fun.

In April 1970, we flew to London, where I was doing my nightclub act at a Chevrolet dealers' convention. Michael bought a beautiful 1970 650cc Triumph Bonneville and had it shipped back to Los Angeles.

We traveled a great deal, to Italy, Germany, France, Jamaica, Hawaii, and Mexico. We also visited Lebanon, where Michael introduced me to his family.

Those were the good times, but I was afraid that, given the disparity in our careers, they wouldn't last forever. Ten years into our marriage, I gave an achingly honest interview to a newspaper journalist about the problems Michael and I encountered in our marriage.

"My husband, Michael," I said, "is becoming more and more annoyed watching me go to work every day while he sits home. He hates the thought of it. I don't blame him. There isn't a man around who enjoys the feeling that his wife is the breadwinner and brings home the bacon. I know it's uncomfortable for Michael. What are we going to do about it? I wish I knew. . . . All I'm sure of is that Michael would give anything to see our positions reversed."

Much later, Michael himself admitted, "I should have known it would be difficult for a man in the business to have a wife who's in the limelight."

Difficult or not, Michael and I had no plans to end our marriage, and we still loved each other as much as we ever had. Then in 1971, to our delight, I became pregnant with our second child. We'd always longed for Matthew to have a sister—so much so that when they wheeled me out of the delivery room after my son's birth, Michael kissed me and said, "So shall we start trying for a girl now?"

My response is unprintable!

But now I was pregnant again. Michael was ecstatic, and so was Matthew, who was excited at the prospect of having a brother (a sister, it seemed, was not on *his* agenda).

I was thrilled, of course, but I was also a little nervous about my pregnancy. After all, I was in my late thirties and exhausted after acting, singing, and dancing nonstop all over the country for so many years. So when I was offered a ten-week tour, first starring in the musical *The Unsinkable Molly Brown* beginning in June and covering St. Louis, Kansas City, and Dallas, then starring in *The Sound of Music,* for once in my life I was overcome by a burning desire to refuse not just one job but two.

But Michael was not working, and if I didn't take this opportunity, our family would go hungry. Although I knew in my heart that this wasn't the case, against my better judgment, I agreed to star in both musicals and tour the country right up until I was eight months pregnant.

Before I left to go on tour, I consulted my doctor, who cautioned me to be careful but didn't insist I stay home. He gave me a list of obstetricians in all the cities where I'd be performing so I could have regular checkups, and off I went, singing and dancing all across America.

It was a grueling schedule and I knew it, but I took heart in the fact that the producer of *The Sound of Music* was John Kenley, the famous summer stock producer who'd worked with Ethel Merman, Marlene Dietrich, Zsa Zsa Gabor, and countless other stars. I'd worked with John before in summer stock and was extremely fond of him. He was a theatrical legend—when he was ninety-nine years old, he could still do spectacular high kicks. When he died in 2009 at one hundred and three, the accolades poured in, praising him for his talent and ingenuity.

But that was only the half of it. The even more sensational story was that he was a hermaphrodite and proud of it. He confided in me that he'd been raised as a boy because his parents had concluded that it would be easier for him to go through life as a male rather than as a female. However, during the rest of his adult life, he chose to spend the winters in Ohio living as a man, and the summers in Palm Springs living as a woman named Joan.

So my ten-week tour of America began. In each town I had a checkup with an obstetrician, and each time I was assured that my baby was fine and I had nothing to be worried about. But as the weeks went by, I began to feel weak and exhausted. Moreover—and this is when I was playing the novice nun Maria in *The Sound of Music*—my bulge was beginning to show. I'll never forget the kindly audience member who waited for me outside the theater after the show and said knowingly, "Be careful, dear, next time you skip down those steps."

By the time the show arrived in Washington, D.C., my feet ached, my back hurt dreadfully, and I was just wiped out with exhaustion. As usual, I had my checkup; the doctor examined me thoroughly, then asked when I was going home. "Pretty soon," I said brightly. I was more than seven months pregnant and the tour was nearly over. In a few weeks I could go home, relax, and have my baby.

When I got home to Los Angeles and saw my regular doctor, he examined me for what seemed like an eternity. Finally he said gently, "Barbara, I think we have a problem."

Now, I've been a positive thinker my entire life. Optimism is bred in my bones, and negativity is as foreign to me as finding a rattlesnake inside a box of chocolates. So I struggled to associate the word "problem" with my much-longed-for baby.

"What kind of problem?" I said finally.

"I'm afraid I can't find a heartbeat," he said very quietly. "But I can't be certain; I can't say anything for sure. You need to immediately go to the hospital and have a sonogram right away."

Like a sleepwalker marooned in the midst of a horrendous nightmare, I went out to the waiting room, where little Matthew was waiting with Michael. My son took one look at my stricken face and cried, "What's the matter, Mommy? What's the matter?"

I couldn't bear to tell him the truth.

"Nothing, Matthew," I said. "Nothing."

Michael and I exchanged covert glances, in which I silently signaled to him how bad things looked for the baby.

But Matthew must have picked up on our signals. He piped up, "Mommy, I *am* going to have a baby brother, aren't I?"

Picking my words extremely carefully, I said, "We're not sure, Matthew, but I think so."

He had never seen me cry in his whole life, and I didn't intend for him to see me crying now, but I was within inches of losing all self-control.

By the time our car pulled up in front of Good Samaritan Hospital, where I had given birth to Matthew and had been so deliriously happy, I was shaking from head to foot and fighting back the tears.

Michael helped me out of the car. My friend Mary was outside the hospital, waiting for me, and so was Michael's mother.

I had been on the road since I'd first found out that I was pregnant, but now my pregnancy was extremely visible. So when I walked into the hospital, the nurses, some of whom who had assisted at Matthew's birth, virtually broke into applause.

"You're having another baby, Miss Eden, how wonderful!" they said in unison.

The only reply I could summon up was, "I'm not sure."

The receptionist presented me with a medical history form to fill out, but my hand shook so much that I almost dropped the pen. So I dictated my answers to the questions to Mary, who wrote them down for me instead.

Then I was taken into a treatment room, where I was hooked up to a machine that beeped in time with a thumping heart. But I could hear only one heart beating, my own. Not a second one. Not my baby's.

It was already achingly obvious to me that my baby was no longer alive. There are no words to express my anguish.

The doctors took X-rays and performed other tests, and then my doctor called me into his office and confirmed what I already knew.

My baby was dead. His umbilical cord had been crushed, and there was nothing anyone could do to save him. I say him, because the doctor told me that my unborn baby was a boy. The doctor also told me that in all his many years of practice, he had never encountered a case like mine. I listened to his words and tried to grasp the meaning, but the only thing that was clear to me was that my baby was dead.

The worst was breaking the news to Matthew that I wasn't going to have a baby and he wasn't going to have a brother. Telling him broke my heart, so much so that even today I have obliterated his reaction from my memory because the torture of recalling it would be unendurable.

As for Michael, his face was ashen with grief. He put his arms around me and hugged me. I could tell that he was stifling his sobs. So was I. But not only that. I was stifling something far worse: the thought that if I'd stayed home during my pregnancy, perhaps the baby could have survived.

At the time, I stopped myself from articulating all those terrible thoughts and did my utmost to sublimate them. But I failed dismally. I've heard a tragedy can bring a couple together, but the death of our second son hurt our relationship beyond repair.

I don't know how the doctors broke the news to me, which words they used, what consolation they attempted to hand me. I only knew that I had to carry my dead baby inside of me for six more weeks, because were the doctors to deliver his lifeless body before then, my own life could be endangered. In hindsight, this is a barbaric, outmoded medical practice, and thankfully it is no longer done.

*   *   *

Everywhere I went, kind, well-meaning fans congratulated me on the upcoming birth of my baby. And when they did, I fixed a rictus of a smile to my face and said nothing. Even when they asked me what I planned to name the baby and what color I was going to paint the nursery, I smiled wanly but said nothing.

I was admitted to the maternity ward of the hospital for the delivery, exactly as if my son had been a full-term baby destined to live. My mother came down from San Franscico to help Michael take care of Matthew.

So, on a date I can't remember, and don't want to, my dead baby was delivered, and I went home without him.

True to form, I threw myself into work and tried hard not to look back. It never occurred to me that I might suffer from postpartum depression. Why should I? After all, I hadn't really had a baby. It was only when I talked to doctors years afterward that I learned that, aside from the heartbreak of having lost my child, because I'd carried him almost to term I had the same hormonal issues as a new mother.

At the time, utterly unaware of this, within days of the delivery I was back in Las Vegas again, rehearsing my brand-new act at the Landmark Hotel, where I was booked to perform for three weeks: two shows a night, seven days a week.

Work had always been my salvation, and I intended to drown myself in the show, in singing. But although I rehearsed and rehearsed and rehearsed, I found that I now had a lot of trouble memorizing the song lyrics, or even focusing on them at all.

A close friend approached me during that period and asked me how I felt after losing my baby, as I seemed to be very happy. My response, "You're right! I'm fine, just fine," I said, then flashed him a radiant smile.

Appearing in Las Vegas is lonely at the best of times, but I now inexplicably craved solitude above all things else. Between shows, it was as if a master hypnotist had lured me into my car and ordered me to drive, because I'd wake up as if from a deep sleep and somehow find myself sitting by the shores of Hoover Dam, staring at the black water, without having a clue about how I arrived and what I was doing or wanted to do there.

My mother flew down from San Francisco to spend time with

me in Las Vegas. She looked at me with the loving yet wise eyes of a parent who knows and understands her daughter better than anyone else in the whole world, and said, "Barbara, you're not well. You're not well at all."

I assured her that I was just fine.

Usually I tended to spend most of my time locked away alone in my dressing room. I'd warm up, do my show, and go straight back to the hotel. I didn't talk at all, hardly ate, and wasn't remotely tempted by even one scoop of ice cream, usually my favorite treat. My weight dropped from my normal 120 pounds to 105 pounds.

After a week, I overheard my mother on the phone saying to my sister, "She's dying, and no one is doing anything about it."

I heard and understood what she was saying. But even the knowledge that she was right couldn't motivate me to try to get help for my condition.

At the end of my three-week engagement at the Landmark, all I wanted to do was go home to Los Angeles, so I raced through the desert at eighty miles an hour. But once I arrived back home, I felt empty, lost, and hopeless, unable to communicate much with Michael or feel close to him anymore. Even Matthew, sweet and loving, failed to mitigate my despair.

Gene had booked me to appear at a nightclub in Puerto Rico, then in a series of Caribbean clubs. Although I didn't want to take the work, I knew that I had no choice. Again, if I didn't work, who would?

Then I developed a really bad cold, and that cold saved my life. I consulted my doctor, and to my puzzlement, he asked me to hold my hand out.

I did and saw that it was shaking.

Up until then, I had truly believed that I was fine, but now I was compelled to face the truth that I was not.

The doctor told Michael that I couldn't work and that it was imperative that I stay home and recuperate. So I did.

But instead of rallying as expected, I plunged into a deep, deep, deep depression. I was clearly in the throes of a classic postpartum depression, except that I didn't have a baby to care for.

Instead, I'd spend hours just sitting in a chair, looking at seven-year-old Matthew, my beautiful little boy, and asking myself why I wasn't happy. I was unable to laugh; I was unable to concentrate on television or on anything else. Sometimes it seemed to me as if I knew exactly what it must feel like to be insane.

My doctor finally diagnosed me as suffering from delayed shock and prescribed me pills to fight it, but they just made me feel even more numb than I had felt before.

Michael and I would meet friends at our favorite ice cream parlor. I'd always loved ice cream, but now, while everybody else had a scoop, all I wanted was a cup of coffee.

I felt nauseous most of the time. I didn't want to hurt myself, but I just had no energy, no interest in anything. My big mistake, of course, was that I should have had counseling, but in those days the very thought of it was anathema to me.

At that crucial stage, Michael and I also should have had joint marital counseling, but that, too, was out of the question. In retrospect, I wish we had.

Instead, Gene came to my rescue with an offer for me to do a musical in the round in Phoenix. Michael asked me if I thought I could do it. I wasn't sure, but I decided to give it a shot anyway, on the condition that he and Matthew come with me. I knew I couldn't be alone anymore, and I was so very relieved when Michael agreed.

However, when I started learning the script, I was disturbed that once again my brain didn't seem to be working as well as before. It was as if I had a barrier there that stopped me from concentrating. I was terrified that I'd forget the words or the dance steps on opening night.

By some miracle, I got through the show without a single hitch. I stayed in it for about three weeks, then went straight back on the road again, doing my nightclub act.

Meanwhile, the rift in my marriage to Michael was growing increasingly wider. As I said before, we should have gone into counseling, not only to cope with our baby's death but also to deal with the growing disparity in our careers and earning power.

Ironically, Michael was filming *Police Story* when I made my decision to end our marriage. That decision was hard and painful, and even now I often question whether it was the right one.

Today, Michael and I have long since found happiness: me with my husband, Jon, and Michael with his wife, Beverly. But I still regret our divorce, because the repercussions it would one day have on Matthew would turn out to be cataclysmic. Had I been able to look into a crystal ball at that time, I would have stayed in the marriage until Matthew was an adult. But I didn't.

It was my decision alone. Michael and I did try to talk about our marital problems, but every time we talked, the chasm between us grew deeper. In the end, he was left angry and bewildered, still not wanting the divorce, insisting that he was happy with me and not understanding my motives for asking for it.

But at the time I was in a deep, dark pit. I was so miserable. I could never quite bring myself to tell Michael the truth: that I had never recovered from the death of my baby. All I wanted was to create a new life for myself. Divorcing Michael seemed to be the only solution.

We finally separated on May 28, 1973, after fifteen years of marriage. At the time, Michael made a statement to the press claiming that he was shocked by our separation. "I don't know what happened. She felt we'd become completely incompatible and there was no point in continuing our marriage," he said. That's exactly what I did say, but, looking back with the hindsight of terrible but real knowledge, I wish to the bottom of my heart that I had not.

****** *chapter 11* ******

CHUCK

* * * * * * * * * * * * *

SOON AFTER MY separation from Michael, I was in the midst of an engagement at the Empire Room of the Palmer House, then Chicago's best and ritziest hotel, when I began receiving flowers. Every single morning, every single evening, there were glorious flowers, with no note—just an elegant card embossed with the initial *C.*

Right from the start, Charles Donald Fegert knew exactly how to treat a lady, or so it seemed at the time. First there were the flowers, then an invitation to a birthday party at the Four Torches, a restaurant, I later discovered, of which he was part owner. I was alone in Chicago and feeling somewhat lonely, so I accepted.

At the restaurant, he was formally introduced to me as Chuck Fegert, vice president of advertising and marketing for the *Chicago Sun-Times* and the *Chicago Daily News.* He was tall, fair, and handsome, and he looked very much like a young Gregory Peck. Even at that early stage, I was wildly attracted to him. A newspaperman, a "civilian," from a world so different from show business, but such a fascinating one!

Yet within a few minutes of our first meeting, his personality began to grate on me, as he moved close—far too close—to me and yelled, "Hey, somebody take a shot of me with my arm around my fantasy dream girl!" My interest in him plummeted. He was rude and aggressive, and although I posed for the photograph, I did it extremely reluctantly. A copy of that photograph is still in existence somewhere around, and the expression on my face—a mixture of distaste and annoyance—says it all.

I had always trusted my first instincts about people, and my first instincts about Chuck were far from positive. Looking back, I only wish I'd followed my gut feelings about him.

But Chuck was completely oblivious to the negative impression he'd made on me. Or, like the best salesmen, who refuse to take no for an answer, he knew but didn't let it deter him one bit. Moreover, he understood exactly how to woo a woman, and he definitely was not a quitter. The flowers kept arriving, and so did the phone calls. And each night, like it or not, I looked out into the audience and there he was, Chuck Fegert, gazing at me with a winning combination of boyish enthusiasm and masculine lust sparkling in his eyes.

Gradually his energetic and enthusiastic courtship of me began to make life seem more exciting and full of promise. His constant presence, his unwavering focus on me at my shows, the flowers, and the phone calls all contributed to eroding my negative first impression of him.

In the end, I agreed to go out on a date with him, and it was then that I discovered that he'd been obsessed with me long before we were first formally introduced in Chicago. Over champagne and caviar (Chuck always had style, I'll grant him that) he told me the story. He'd been staying in the Beverly Hills Hotel, and I was in the lobby with Gene. As he remembered it, I was very, very tanned (I'd just come back from Acapulco) and was wearing white hip-huggers. From that moment on, he designated me his "fantasy girl."

Warning bells should have gone off in my head then, but I was so dazzled by Chuck's physical presence, his silver-tongued flattery, that I let down my defenses. Besides, he exuded power, strength, and commitment. Whatever I did seemed to enchant him, and he continually showered me with praise and made me feel as if I were the most important woman in the world to him.

Michael and I were separated, our divorce was immment, and I was, quite simply, lonely. And having Chuck around made life seem more lighthearted, easier, and more complete.

We started exchanging confidences, hopes, dreams, and, as lovers usually do, histories. I discovered that he had been born in Chicago, the son of a steelworker, and that his first job was in the mills. Switching gears, he took a degree in business administration, then got a job in advertising and marketing at the *Chicago Sun-Times*. There, with his style, creativity, energy, and charisma, he made an instant impact, and was quickly promoted.

Married twice, the second time to a top model, he had a photographic memory, and had his fingers in many lucrative pies (including oil wells and discos). He was a true swashbuckler and a heartbreaker to boot.

Foolish as it may seem in light of what would transpire between us, I began to feel that Chuck might very well turn out to be my happily-ever-after, a safe haven at last.

Soon I was involved deeply enough to invite Chuck to be my date at Dean Martin's opening at the MGM Grand in Las Vegas. There we were snapped by a tabloid photographer, with me, as the caption says, "snuggling up" to Chuck.

I suppose I was. He was sexy, intelligent, charismatic, full of energy, and determined to make me his, no matter what it took. And, at forty-six to my thirty-nine, he was a grown-up. Or rather, that's what I assumed.

Before I knew it, I was head over heels in love with Chuck and seriously pondering the wisdom of creating a future with him. Then, just after my divorce from Michael became final, Chuck casually announced that he was married.

We'd been dating eight months. During that time he'd been away on various business trips, but I'd never dreamed there was anyone else, least of all a wife.

I was shocked and angry, but Chuck assured me that he and his wife were separated and that their divorce was imminent. Smooth and persuasive as ever, he somehow contrived to make me forget that for eight whole months, he hadn't mentioned that he was married.

My mother, however, did not forget at all. She and Chuck met when I was performing in San Francisco. Normally Chuck, a consummate salesman, could charm the socks right off anyone from the very first moment, but my mother remained utterly impervious to his blandishments. When all was said and done, all his gifts given, all his flowery compliments paid, my mother still didn't like Chuck one bit and made absolutely no bones about it.

No matter how hard he tried to get her to like him, she would just sit there, puff on her cigarette, and say, "Oh, really?" then turn to talk to someone else. She refused to ever let the name "Chuck" pass her lips, and forever afterward would refer to him only as "what's-his-name."

Besotted as I was, there were moments when even I had my doubts about him. Although I found his forcefulness alluring, I was uncomfortable with his relentless name-dropping. Chuck routinely reminded practically everyone he rubbed shoulders with about his stellar connections. It was Ronnie (Reagan) one minute, Frank (Sinatra) the next. Of course, he did know Ronald Reagan and Frank Sinatra, but not quite as well as he made out. This didn't endear him to many people and, I was afraid, probably caused them to make fun of him behind his back. But if he knew, I don't think he cared. He found fame by association so very dazzling.

*

I did meet Sinatra through him, though, when we went to a dinner at Sinatra's house in Palm Springs. Mr. Sinatra was lovely to me, although clearly a man's man who much preferred the company of other men to that of women.

I never met President Reagan with Chuck at all. I did with Michael, however, when we attended his inaugural ball, and twice after that, once with a boyfriend, and then with my husband, Jon. To me, Reagan looked like a businessman. A big man in a big coat.

On the subject of presidents, when I was working at the Fairmont Hotel in Atlanta, future president Jimmy Carter, then governor of Georgia, came to see the show with his daughter, Amy. After the show, he invited me to the governor's mansion, where I met his wife, Rosalynn. Amy was jumping around on the furniture, eating an orange—sweet, innocent, and unaffected.

Still worse than Chuck's name-dropping was his continual drive to be the center of attention, his constant and overweening need for applause. Before we met, he had been a popular after-dinner speaker. Now that we were an item, the demand for him to perform speaking engagements increased, and Chuck loved it. His yearning to be onstage at all times was such that I sometimes caught myself wondering if he was the actor, not me.

The truth was that *he* wanted to be the star. Looking back, I see that although he was a brilliant man and a talented salesman, Chuck was very insecure. He was like a spoiled child who wanted to hog all the attention and couldn't endure it if he didn't get it. He just had to entertain at all costs, even if the jokes he cracked constantly weren't funny.

The problem was that I was the entertainer, not him, and in his heart he knew it and resented me. And the longer we spent together, the stronger his resentment. In fact, one of his favorite quotes, which he later served out with relish to journalists who asked him about our marriage, was, "Before I met her, I always told jokes at parties and had developed a reputation as an emcee and raconteur. Now people come up to her and say, 'Hey, aren't you the famous Barbara Fegert?'"

All my doubts aside, I was in love with Chuck and he with me, and soon I was dividing my time between Los Angeles and Chuck's luxurious apartment on the forty-second floor of the Water Tower. He had a bachelor pad with spectacular views of the lake and the glittering lights of the city below.

The apartment boasted a bedroom with mirrored ceilings and a Jacuzzi. Chuck was so proud of that bedroom, because it epitomized the playboy image he always tried so hard to project (not that it was entirely false). Many of his friends were playboys, late-night parties were de rigueur for him, and whenever Sinatra was in town (which was often), he and Chuck hung out together.

At the start of our relationship, I commuted between LA and Chicago, and Chuck did the same, later grousing that he had made the trip thirty-one times. Then, in the same breath, he'd boast to the press, "Barbara is such an old-fashioned girl, she refuses to live with me. Her values are so traditional."

From the first, part of the problem was that I still wanted to work, and work I did. We tried to spend as much time as possible together, but I kept being offered jobs, and I took them, not just because I loved working but also because I didn't want to put my life on hold and become a stay-at-home wife. That wasn't whom Chuck had fallen in love with or who I intrinsically am. But the reality was that while Chuck loved to have me work, he also hated it because it took time away from him, and also because, no matter how hard I tried not to, I inevitably upstaged him.

I told myself that because my career made Chuck feel so insecure, the only solution was for me to marry him. That way, I reasoned, he would know that we were a unit, a couple, and then he'd be secure, settled, and content and we'd go on and have a good life together.

So although I was riddled with doubts about the wisdom of what I was about to do, I agreed to marry Chuck. The wedding took place in a storybook setting: a lakeside horse ranch, with a large main house, owned by one of Chuck's friends. Unfortunately, I was one and a half hours late for my own wedding. Not that it was my fault (the hairdresser driving me there got lost), but in retrospect, it seems symbolic.

Despite my mother's distaste for Chuck, she still attended the wedding, though afterward she sniffed, "He acted like the bride, not the groom." At that point, I was still far too loyal to Chuck to ask her exactly what she meant by that remark.

But even without her spelling it out, I knew that, unlike Michael, Chuck was not good husband material. Everything about Chuck was the opposite of Michael Ansara, with his honesty, his integrity, his steadfastness. Chuck was all about frivolity, excitement, and drama.

By then, I knew his character. I knew that he could be mean, but I didn't quite accept it, and blamed myself instead. I thought that his unkindness to Matthew and his friends, his controlling way with me, were all down to the fact that he wasn't used to living with a career woman.

Matthew didn't warm to my new husband, either. He was nine when I first met Chuck. Soon after, Chuck and I took his two children and Matthew to a Nevada dude ranch for a vacation. We rode horses and had fun. But when I broke the news to Matthew that I was marrying Chuck and that we very much wanted him to be part of the wedding, his answer was brief and to the point.

"Oh boy! We're going to have trouble with Daddy."

Trouble?

I dug deeper and got the real story out of Matthew. Michael had made it clear to our son that if I married Chuck, he didn't want Matthew to live with us in Chicago; rather, he wanted him to stay in Los Angeles with him.

I prepared for battle and contacted my attorney, Joe Taback. To my surprise, Joe suggested that I take a meeting with Michael's attorney.

In advance of the meeting, I consulted a child psychologist, who confirmed my deepest fears at the time: experts firmly believed that it was better for a teenage boy to live with his father, not his mother.

Perhaps. But not in my case, I told myself. Not in my case, given all the love I possessed for Matthew, how much I adored him, and how I lived to make him happy. Besides, I was his mother, and no man could ever compete with that.

I arrived at the meeting with all guns blazing, my attorney by my side, ready to battle to the death for custody of Matthew.

So I was floored when Michael's attorney greeted us with the announcement that *Matthew* wanted to live with Michael, not vice versa. I didn't believe him. Then he produced a letter in Matthew's childlike writing.

I want to live with my daddy, it said, almost breaking my heart.

I left the office in tears and rushed home to talk to Matthew. I wanted to find out what had prompted his decision, and how much pressure his father had put on him to make it.

At the same time, I was determined to be understanding. I took one look at his face and saw how crushed and hurt he was, how tragically his loyalties were divided between Michael and me. That was my worst nightmare. So I kissed him and said, "Don't worry, Matthew. It's all right, it's your daddy, and of course you want to live with him. I understand."

From then on, I did and said what I thought was best for

Matthew, no matter how tough that was for me. I believed that a good parent shouldn't put an innocent child in the middle of a conflict between a mother and a father, and I lived up to my beliefs, no matter how much it killed me emotionally.

Back in Chicago, Chuck still wanted to promote his playboy image, despite the fact that he now had a wife. To that end, when the *Chicago Sun-Times* came to photograph us for a feature, he insisted that I be photographed in a bubble bath, while he lounged next to me in a cherry-red satin dressing gown, Hugh Hefner style.

They say that the universe sometimes sends you subtle—and not-so-subtle—signals that show you what is really going on in your life, if only you pay attention. And I believe that what happened next was the perfect example.

Just before Christmas, I was in the elevator, taking the dry cleaning downstairs, when all of a sudden the elevator ground to a halt between floors. Then it began bouncing up and down frighteningly fast.

Someone once told me that if an elevator drops, you should lie flat on the floor, so that you can protect your spine and spread the shock when the elevator hits the ground. So that's what I did: I threw myself onto the elevator floor.

Just then I heard a cable snap. Then another one. I reached up and pushed the emergency button, trying hard not to panic. As I did, I felt the elevator drop further. All I could think of was the movie *The Towering Inferno*, and I prayed.

Then I heard more cables unravel, and the sound of the broken pieces tumbling down the shaft. I held my breath. Would the elevator itself be next?

There was another shudder; the elevator dropped once more and then ground to a halt.

I spent the next ninety-three minutes cowering on the elevator floor, trapped.

Finally the door was yanked open and I was helped out onto the thirty-second floor, where the elevator had stopped. As the elevator repairman helped me out, he took one look at my ashen face and yelled, "Jeannie! Why didn't you get yourself out?" I almost socked him.

But what I didn't recognize until later was that the universe was signaling me big-time.

In 1978, soon after Chuck and I married, I was cast as Stella Johnson, owner of La Moderna Beauty Parlor, in my first major movie role in fourteen years, *Harper Valley PTA*. The movie was inspired by the hit Jeannie C. Riley song, written by Tom T. Hall, but the film had echoes of *Peyton Place* as well.

Stella, an unconventional single mom, wore short skirts, drank beer, and wasn't afraid to speak her mind, frequently embarrassing her young daughter. The turning point in the script came when the Harper Valley PTA vented their disapproval of Stella on her daughter, whereupon an outraged Stella stormed into the PTA and gave them a piece of her mind.

The movie was low-budget, filmed on location in southern Illinois. I hadn't realized that part of Illinois is virtually a part of the South, and the people there speak with a southern accent. But low-budget or not, *Harper Valley PTA* proved to be a surprise box office success.

Consequently, in 1981, NBC decided to create a TV series based on the movie, which was shot at Universal. It started out being a lot of fun. Matthew, now sixteen, appeared in one episode, in the role of a high school student.

Michael came over to the set and coached Matthew in his part because he was so nervous about his acting ability. I was also a basket case at the prospect of acting in a scene with my son, although he only had three lines to say, but he did very well in the part and I was vastly relieved.

*

The first year of the series went well, because we had wonderful producers—Sherwood Schwartz and his son, Lloyd. Then NBC decided they wanted to make a change, and brought in a new production team, which included a couple of guys who seemed to think that smoking pot was the way to make a hit series. I've never been judgmental about drugs, but the continual smell grossed me out.

After I reported them, they took their pot smoking elsewhere, but the fallout from their behavior was that the series suffered considerably and after two years and twenty-nine episodes was canceled.

One good thing that came out of *Harper Valley PTA* is that I was able to buy a beautiful four-bedroom home high above Beverly Hills with a spectacular view of the city, an infinity pool, and a library. When I first moved into the house, it had an overwhelming preponderance of dark wood. I tore down walls, created windows, replaced the floor with hardwood, made one bedroom into an office, and had most of the house decorated in peach, blue, and green—all happy colors. My living room and my bedroom are mirrored to reflect the outdoors.

During my brief stays in Chicago, to Chuck's dismay, I became somewhat of a local celebrity. The columns seemed to follow my activities incessantly. I joined the board of a major Chicago bank (a kick, considering that I'd once worked as a humble bank employee in San Francisco) and socialized with friends, including the columnist Irv Kupcinet, whose wife, Essee, used to cook us delicious homestyle meals.

During that time, Matthew came to visit. He got on well with Chuck's daughter, but Chuck did his utmost to divide us. He didn't want Matthew to love me, or anyone else to even like me. I could see that, but instead of fighting back, I grew very quiet and withdrawn, far from the bright, happy, effervescent woman Chuck had first met and professed to love.

*

The last straw was when, after we had planned to take a long summer vacation together, I received an offer to star in *The Best Little Whorehouse in Texas* and accepted it without consulting Chuck about my decision. In retrospect, I realize that, in the interests of keeping my husband happy, I probably shouldn't have taken the job, but the part was good, and I really wanted to do the show.

Chuck was livid. Increasingly, he did all he could to put me down whenever the opportunity arose.

He was rude, controlling, and virulently competitive with me. For example, one evening, a maitre d' welcomed me at a restaurant. Chuck erupted in fury and yelled, "I'm the one who pays the bill. He should greet me, not you!" A minor incident, but indicative of Chuck's bitter mind-set and innate dissatisfaction with me and with our marriage.

One night we went to see Richard Burton in *Camelot*, then playing in Chicago. I'd loved Richard Burton ever since seeing him in *The Robe* (in which, incidentally, Michael also appeared), and I was excited to see him onstage in person.

I loved the show, but Chuck yawned loudly most of the way through the first act. As soon as the curtain came down for the interval, he got up, grabbed my arm, and said, "Come on, Barbara, we're leaving!"

I was mortified, both because I was enjoying the show so much and because I was acutely aware of how big a snub it is to an actor if someone leaves the theater before the play is over, particularly if that person is someone you know. Although we hadn't yet met Richard Burton, we had mutual friends, and we were scheduled to have dinner with Richard and his wife, Suzy, after the show.

"We can't walk out in the middle of the show, Chuck," I said. "Richard Burton will realize and be devastated."

Chuck snorted. "Don't be so vain, Barbara. You think you're

so important? Look at how many people there are in the audience. Burton won't give you a single thought. And he certainly won't notice that you've walked out."

Crushed, just as he had intended, I gave in, and we left the theater.

A couple of hours later, we met Richard and Suzy at the designated restaurant for dinner, as arranged.

We had hardly sat down when Richard flashed me an accusatory look with those searing blue eyes, which could burn through your heart and soul.

"I'm so sorry you left the show at the interval, Barbara. You missed the whole second act," he said.

I could have curled up and died, I felt so horrible. I was so ashamed, and spent the rest of the evening tongue-tied and humiliated while Chuck told anecdote after anecdote, the life of the party.

Our marriage clearly was on a collision course with disaster. Chuck grew to resent me more and more, and relished telling me in one breath how much he hated me and in the next how much he loved me. He was aggressive, erratic, out of control. It took me much too long to register that he was abusing alcohol and cocaine.

The signs were all there: the rage, the paranoia, the hypersexuality. One night he came home late after partying most of the evening. I was already in bed, and because I didn't want any scenes, I pretended to be fast asleep. In the dark, I heard Chuck stumble into my special makeup chair and then fling it across the room.

In the morning, while Chuck got ready for work, I kept my eyes firmly shut, feigning deep sleep. He made no attempt to wake me. After he left, I showered and got dressed, then cast around for my makeup chair, but it was nowhere to be seen.

I spent the next hour scouring our three-thousand-square-foot apartment from floor to ceiling, and finally found my makeup chair on a high ledge above the guest room closet, where Chuck had obviously hidden it. A cruel practical joke, and a lesson: everything that I cared about, everything I needed, was unimportant to him, and needed to be damaged or thrown away.

Night after night, he was out partying, and when he came home, if I was still awake, he would taunt me: "I'm glad you didn't go because you're so dull. You're no fun at a party. No one wants you around because they don't like you."

Another night, he came home late while I was fast asleep, and shook me awake.

"Get up, Barbara, you're taking up too much room in bed!" he yelled at the top of his voice.

I refused. We had words. Then he kicked me so hard that I fell on the floor. But instead of whimpering, I dusted myself off, picked up a book, locked myself in the bathroom, and stayed there all night, reading, while Chuck banged on the door relentlessly, yelling for me to come out.

Through all the noise and the banging, the name-calling and the abuse, I just kept on reading. When dawn broke, gambling on the strong possibility that Chuck was now sleeping the pill-induced sleep of someone coming down from a cocaine high, I crept out of the bathroom and into the living room.

I sat there on the couch, having a silent dialogue with myself.

You're insane, Barbara Eden. Why are you doing this? Why are you staying married to a man you don't even want to be in the same room with?

Then I got up, got dressed, took a cab to the storage facility filled with all my things that hadn't yet been delivered to the apartment, and had them shipped back to Los Angeles. Then I headed back to the apartment. It was afternoon by the time I got there. I packed my suitcases and called to make airline reservations.

*

As fate would have it, all flights between Chicago and Los Angeles were booked for that night, so I got myself a ticket on the first plane that was scheduled to leave the next morning.

Then I heard the door open. It was Chuck. A clever man, with good instincts, he'd come home from work early. Then the sales talk began.

"I love you, Barbara Jean, I love you," he kept saying, over and over. He called me Barbara Jean because he knew my family had always called me that, and he believed that if he also used that name, it would give him power over me.

"I love you, Barbara Jean. I've never loved anybody like you, never," he said, over and over.

I didn't believe him, and yet . . . For a little while longer, I was sold on him again. After all, he was my husband, I still loved him, and so I stayed.

On New Year's Eve, I had to work at the Fontainebleau in Miami Beach, and Chuck flew down to Florida to be with me. When I first found out that he was coming, I wasn't completely bowled over by his devotion, as I knew that he had close friends down there and was keen to party with them. However, I abandoned my misgivings and let my guard slip after he promised to be in the audience.

That night, I was happy at the prospect of him seeing me in the show, and I had just finished applying my makeup and was about to go onstage when the phone rang. Without any preamble, Chuck announced that he wouldn't be in the audience after all. There was no explanation, no excuse. The disappointment was so sharp that it felt as if Chuck was stabbing me in the heart with a rusty bread knife. Too dispirited to argue, I hung up and did my show anyway.

At the back of my mind was the nagging question of why Chuck hadn't invited me to join him after the show was over, no matter how late that might be. But instead of moping around, I reminded myself that it was New Year's Eve and accepted an invitation to a party given by our friends Charlie and Rusty Stein.

I was doing my utmost to join in the spirit of the night and have a good time when, out of the blue, some supposedly well-meaning woman suddenly blurted out how lucky Chuck was to be invited to Sinatra's party that night. So now I knew the truth—my husband had chosen Frank Sinatra over me. Even worse, as I later discovered, he had taken one of his former wives, the beautiful model, along with him as well, and that hurt.

But heartbroken as I was, I carried on partying with the Steins and their friends. After all, it was New Year's Eve. Besides, I've always believed in not betraying my deepest emotions to anyone. In fact, you could say that the song "Don't Cry Out Loud" was written with me in mind.

I was due to host the Orange Bowl Parade, then be introduced during halftime at the game. As a conciliatory gesture, I agreed to go with Chuck to a party that was being thrown at an elegant, multimillion-dollar Turnberry Isle apartment later that day.

When I got there, everyone was partying as if there were no tomorrow. Still, the hosts had made an attempt to give a formal dinner, at which I was seated next to the wife of a big Florida developer. I glanced out onto the terrace, just in time to see the developer in the throes of a passionate kiss with another woman. I looked back at his wife's face, saw her glassy eyes, and realized that she didn't even register her husband's infidelity. It was as if a veil had been ripped from in front of my eyes. The entire room was zonked out of their minds on coke.

At last I faced the facts. This place and these people were not for me. More to the point, neither was my husband or our marriage. And I couldn't believe that it had taken me so long to see the light.

Fortunately, the party was in full swing, and the noise was so loud that no one noticed when I crept out of the room and upstairs to the guest bedroom, where I'd left my Louis Vuitton suitcases.

Exhausted by my dreadful night at Turnberry Isle, my revulsion at all the drug use and carousing going on, and Chuck's indifference to me, I lay down on the bed. Before I knew it, I drifted off to sleep.

When I opened my eyes again, dawn was breaking. No one had come to find me, no one knew where I was, and no one cared, least of all my husband. I buzzed the doorman to come get my luggage.

Then the bedroom door opened, and there was Chuck, wasted from a night of drinking and drugs. He stood there staring at me intently, tall and handsome despite the ravages of alcohol and cocaine. He must have seen something flicker in my expression, because he walked over to the bed, almost like a sleepwalker, sat down, rested his head in his hands, and said, "I'm so sorry, Barbara Jean, I'm so sorry."

I took one look at my husband, the man I had once thought I loved with all my heart, and simply walked out, my head held high, and didn't look back.

Chuck merely watched as I left. He knew it was over between us and that any attempt to persuade me otherwise would be futile.

I took a cab to the airport and flew home to Los Angeles, alone. I felt sad that I no longer loved Chuck, and depressed that I was about to go through another divorce, but at least our split was my choice, and I was convinced that it was absolutely the right one.

****** *chapter 12* ******

FREE AGAIN

* * * * * * * * * * * * * *

FORTUNATELY, IMMEDIATELY AFTER my split from Chuck, I was able to drown any vestiges of melancholy in my new role as the madam in a touring company of the musical *The Best Little Whorehouse in Texas.* Moreover, my mother had moved down to LA from San Francisco and was now living with me, so I had her for company, which made life pleasanter and less lonely.

I loved the script, the songs, and everything else about *The Best Little Whorehouse in Texas,* with just one exception: that four-letter word starting in *f* and ending in *k,* which the madam, my character in the show, uses frequently. My mother and I pored over the script together and spent hours trying to come up with alternative words to replace that dreaded one, but to no avail.

Finally the director laid down the law and in his Texas accent ruled, "Barbara Jean, just please say the word."

And that, as they say, was that. So although I blushed a little on opening night, as the tour progressed I became more and more accustomed to using the *f*-word without blushing. And I have to confess that today you could say that I employ it frequently. However, when I do, I try to remember to make a mental apology to my mother, wherever she is. And I sincerely hope that she forgives me.

Soon after I was in *The Best Little Whorehouse in Texas,* Michele Lee, of *Knots Landing* fame, who was married to the actor James Farentino, introduced me to Brentwood plastic surgeon Stanley Frileck, who was also director of the Michael Jackson Burn Center in Culver City.

Stanley was a kind and gentle man, and we struck up a congenial relationship, which then blossomed into a romance; eventually he moved in with me. Fortunately, Matthew liked Stanley a great deal, and, thank the Lord, so did my mother. I felt blessed that Stanley was around to support me during her illness and after her death from lung cancer.

That final illness was cruelly drawn out and caused her a great deal of pain and suffering. I later learned through one of her friends that she had been having difficulty breathing at night for a very long time beforehand, but she continued to ignore her symptoms, and never gave me a clue, either. My guess is that she simply followed her own dictate and rose right above it—until, of course, it was impossible for her to do so anymore.

My mother passed away in November 1986, and I continue to miss her today more than I could ever say. When she lived with me, when I was working, each morning, she would take Matthew to school—Buckley, a private school, and to and from sports practice. And when Matthew was with his father (with whom I thankfully shared joint custody), she and I would go on fun and adventurous trips together, sometimes work-related, other times not.

Everywhere we traveled, even Australia and Fiji, my mother picked up a rock as a souvenir of where we'd been together and what a great time we'd had there. I labeled her souvenirs "Mommy Rocks." Many a suspicious customs officer examined them, picked them up, turned them over, tapped them on the table, and rubbed their rough surfaces, utterly bemused. However, after hearing my mother's wide-eyed explanation, the customs officers grinned, nodded, and let us through.

Stanley and I were together for seven years, but neither of us was passionate enough about the other to take the ultimate step of getting married. After all, I'd been married twice, and I told myself that trying marriage for a third time was a recipe for disaster. So Stanley and I broke up. And guess who is the current love of his life? None other than Michele Lee, who introduced us to each other in the first place. Hollywood musical chairs, you could call it.

* * *

I spent a great many years working on a long series of made-for-television movies, some fun, others not, some worthwhile, others patently not. We can take a whistle-stop tour of some of them.

In 1974 I appeared in a real howler of a TV movie of the week, *The Stranger Within,* in which I gave birth to an alien baby, ate a great deal of raw meat, and drank a lot of coffee. Sigmund Freud probably would have had a field day analyzing that script!

In 1977, I worked on *Stonestreet: Who Killed the Centerfold Model?* (a pilot that, ultimately, did not get sold), playing an undercover cop. My sister, Alison, was an extra. Alison also stood in for me in some of my other movies, not because she wanted to be an actress but because my mother was dying and we both knew that Alison and me working together would make her so happy.

In the *Stonestreet* script my character went undercover as a hooker, plying her trade in a very rough part of LA. I wore a red wig, a minuscule skirt, a plunging top, and towering stilettos.

As I sashayed along Hollywood Boulevard for a long shot, a white Cadillac screeched to a halt beside me. A man leaned out of the window, beckoned, and said, "Get in, honey."

I gave him a wide smile and said, "Not right now. You're on *Candid Camera!*"

He tore away as if the cops were after him.

Later that day, they shot me walking down another stretch of Hollywood Boulevard, past a peep show. In the middle of the shot, a man ducked out of the peep show and ruined the entire scene.

The infuriated director yelled, "Cut!" but the poor man was frozen to the spot.

The director went to war. "If you don't move right now, I'll print it and send a copy to your mother," he said.

The terrified man scurried off like a bunny rabbit pursued by a pack of ravenous wolves.

Watching the scene was a young actress who was playing a ticket booth attendant and had only one line in the movie. Even then, with a faint smile playing on her unusually attractive face, there was a memorable quality about her that was impossible to ignore. When we wrapped for the night, she came over to me and said, "Miss Eden, I really don't know whether or not I want to carry on in this business."

I gave her a few words of encouragement about her acting career, which in essence delivered the message, *Don't give up. Carry on!*

And carry on Ellen Barkin did. She went on to make *The Big Easy* and *Sea of Love,* carving out a stellar movie career for herself. To top that, in her private life, she married and divorced one of the wealthiest men in America. Not bad for a girl who wanted to give up acting all those years ago.

In 1981, I appeared in *Return of the Rebels* with Don Murray, in which the young Patrick Swayze had a small part. He was gentlemanly and polite to me, and I was struck by how close he was to his family and how whenever they came to visit him on the set, he was so warm and kind to them. Patrick was a good guy, and his death from pancreatic cancer at the age of fifty-seven was tragic.

In 1985, NBC ordered a two-hour *I Dream of Jeannie* sequel, *I Dream of Jeannie: 15 Years Later,* in which I played both Jeannie and her evil sister (I always loved playing the sister because, as they say, the devil always gets the best lines).

This time around Sidney Sheldon wasn't available to take creative control of the movie, as by then his career as a novelist was well under way, with books like *The Other Side of Midnight* selling in the millions.

Larry also didn't appear in *I Dream of Jeannie: 15 Years Later,* for the very good reason that *Dallas* was now a massive hit and a cultural phenomenon, and he didn't want to switch horses in midrace, as it were. So Wayne Rogers played Tony, and was very good in the part, although very different from Larry. Wayne, who starred in the hit TV series *M*A*S*H* and then went on to become an investment broker and a financial commentator on TV, nowadays manages my money!

However, donning my Jeannie costume once more after an interval of fifteen years was a very strange feeling. The moment I put it on, I got goose bumps all over my body. I looked in the mirror and felt as though time hadn't passed at all.

The plot of the movie was a bit strange, but probably appropriate for its time. When the story opens, Jeannie has at last realized her own value. She's married to Major Nelson, has a child with him (played by Mackenzie Astin, the twelve-year-old son of Patty Duke and John Astin), and has become more assertive than she was at the start of the series. Deciding that Major Nelson is taking her too much for granted, she moves out of their house, rents an apartment on her own, and attempts to live the life of a 1980s liberated woman. Not the world's most scintillating script, but a worthwhile and fun exercise in nostalgia.

Moreover, two good things emerged out of the show for me. First, I was allowed to display my belly button at last! And *I Dream of Jeannie: 15 Years Later* placed a close second to a World Series game in the ratings, to become the eleventh-highest-rated television movie of 1985.

In 1987, I was cast as Laura Harding in *The Stepford Children*. It was not a particularly thrilling experience. The script featured a robot clone of me. So I had to spend four hours wearing a leotard and stockings, covered in plaster, with straws inserted into my nostrils so I could breathe.

My mother had just died, and my sister, Alison, was working as my double. Both she and I were extremely uncomfortable when we discovered that we had a big scene to shoot in a cemetery. But work is work, so we gritted our teeth and got through the scene, trying hard to forget about our mother's recent burial and concentrate on the action.

A happier experience was the TV movie *Your Mother Wears Combat Boots,* in which I worked with Matthew, then twenty-four. I was playing a woman whose husband was killed in Vietnam after his parachute failed to open during a crucial jump. Years later, the son she had with him is in his late teens and she believes that he is in college. However, to her deep distress, she discovers that he has secretly joined the army instead.

We filmed at Fort Benning, in Georgia. My scene with Matt went like this: I'm dragging my duffle bag across the grounds when Matt comes riding by on a bike. I ask him to direct me to a particular building. Then Matt comes out with his one and only line in

*

the movie: "The white one!" Ever the proud mother, I thought he delivered his one line with a great deal of presence.

The whole shoot presented an extreme physical challenge for me, as the script called for me to undertake a series of parachute jumps. It was scary, but I wanted to prove that I could do it. I worked alongside soldiers, who put me through a parachute training course. It was fun but nerve-racking.

Finally the great day came on which the result of my parachute training was due to be immortalized on film. Feeling strong and brave, I braced myself to climb up three towers, each higher than the last.

I scrambled up the first rickety wooden tower with nary a second's thought, and certainly not even a smidgen of fear. Once I reached the top, a harness was hooked onto my back, I jumped off, the parachute opened, and I floated down to the ground. I did that once. Then, brave as anything, and following the script to the letter, I moved over to the next tower and parachuted off there as well.

Then I got to the third and highest tower. At the base I hesitated for a second, and the sergeant watching said, "You sure you're up for this?"

"Of course I am," I said indignantly.

But the sergeant persisted. "You mean you don't want a double?"

"Well, I did climb the other two," I said, and looked at the sergeant questioningly.

"Are you sure you don't want a double?" he repeated.

I shook my head and started climbing. Three-quarters of the way up the tower, I looked down and saw that the other two towers were below me. As I did, the tower started to sway in the wind.

"You want a double?" the sergeant yelled.

I certainly did!

My next TV outing proved to be frightening as well, but in a very different way: a role in four episodes of *Dallas,* starring, of course, none other than Larry Hagman.

While Larry and I hadn't been in touch much in the intervening years since we were together on *I Dream of Jeannie,* I had watched with a combination of awe and pleasure as Larry's J. R. Ewing became the stuff of which TV history was made. When J.R. was shot in March 1980, a record 350 million viewers throughout the world tuned in, then united in global speculation regarding the identity of his killer.

Naturally, Larry joined in the heated debate, too, his tongue firmly in his cheek. Not even he knew who really shot J.R., as the producers had cunningly opted to shoot several alternative endings to the episode in which the killer was unmasked, each one featuring a different killer. The speculation reached such a feverish height that bookies all over the world made a terrific amount of money from all the people placing bets on the identity of the man—or woman—who had shot J.R.

Funnily enough, when pushed to make a guess about the identity of his would-be assassin, Larry finally said: "Barbara Eden did it!" I was flattered that he thought of me, but couldn't quite ignore the subtext inherent in his casting me as a killer. At the same time, given Larry's off-set demands and the villainy of his on-camera character, I couldn't help gleefully recalling his insistence at not being viewed as the bad guy in *I Dream of Jeannie.*

As it turned out, *I* was going to be the villain this time around, as my character, the dastardly Lee Ann De La Vega, screamed double-crossing diva. According to the script, J.R. did Lee Ann wrong when they were at college together: she became pregnant and he ditched her, after which she had an abortion that almost killed her. Now that she had become rich beyond her wildest dreams, her primary goal in life was to wreak revenge on J.R. and pay him back roundly for all his past iniquities.

An archvillainess, she actually succeeded in taking over Ewing Oil, then engineering the situation so that J.R.'s fiancée, Vanessa, broke off their engagement and walked out on him. Lee Ann's revenge was complete.

When I arrived at the studio on my first day, I was shaking with nerves, not just because I would be working with Larry again after all those years, but also because when you take a role in an established series, you feel like a blundering outsider and ache to fit in with the rest of the cast, but worry that you may not.

That the *Dallas* producers had cast me as Lee Ann with their collective tongue very firmly in cheek became highly obvious the moment I arrived at wardrobe and discovered that my first outfit was a pink suit. Pink! Hardly a subtle reminder of Jeannie.

Larry, I knew, *didn't* want to be reminded of *I Dream of Jeannie*. He'd made that very clear to me throughout the years, not wanting to take part in any *I Dream of Jeannie* retrospectives or *I Dream of Jeannie*-related talk shows (except one joint appearance on *Today*) and doing his utmost to distance himself from the show whenever he was interviewed.

So as I waited to shoot the first scene in which Larry and I were scheduled to act together, I was quaking in my pink high heels. I thought maybe the sight of me might cause him to suddenly implode.

My first entrance was scripted so that I stalk straight out of an elevator and come face-to-face with J.R. So there I was in my pink suit, the elevator door opened, and Larry cracked, "Oh my God! We're going back in time!" I never discovered whether or not that line was part of the script or one that Larry had improvised himself. After all, this was *his* show and he finally had carte blanche to rewrite the script whenever and however he wanted, so I wouldn't have been at all surprised if he had taken advantage of it. Either way, that line was a good one.

Whether intentionally or by accident, whether Larry had any input into it or not, the script of my episode seemed to be full of double entendres that harked back to *I Dream of Jeannie*. In one instance, J.R. takes one look at me and asks, "Haven't we met somewhere before?" Looking at Larry across the set, I really did suddenly experience the weirdest sensation, as if we had indeed gone back in time together. My favorite out of the four *Dallas* episodes I appeared in was episode 343. Wearing a long blond wig fixed with a pink bandeau, I reminisce about how wonderful it was dating J.R. in my youth. Then I switch gears and talk about the shock of revealing my pregnancy to him and his subsequent reaction: denying that he was the father and wanting nothing to do with me.

Then I describe my horrific abortion done by a butcher of a doctor in a cheap, tawdry hotel, how I almost died, and how, as a result, I was forced to quit college. "I don't just want to get back at him," I declare, venom dripping from my every word. "I'm going to change his life totally, just like he once changed mine." Melodramatic in the extreme, my role was a gift to an actress, and I loved playing it.

The shows all went well; I very much enjoyed working with Patrick Duffy, and both Larry and Linda Gray were extremely nice to me. Even better, the fans seemed happy that Larry and I had reunited, if only for four episodes.

Despite some of the more bizarre past memories of Larry, I still thought of him fondly, and was gratified that he had met with such stratospheric success in *Dallas*. The series would run for a record fourteen seasons, from 1978 to 1991, and along the way, Larry could hardly have been blamed for having acquired some starlike mannerisms and demands. He'd been waiting to become a star for so long and was clearly primed to enjoy every moment of his stardom.

However, I was a little surprised, not to say shocked, when my friend Dolores came to visit the *Dallas* set, and beforehand was briefed by one of Larry's people that she was not permitted to talk to him unless he addressed her first, nor was she allowed to look at him.

That same year, I made *I Still Dream of Jeannie,* an NBC movie of the week. This time, the plot has Major Nelson spirited away into space on an extended secret mission, leaving Jeannie on earth. There, her jealous sister—as always, feverishly working against her—insists on enforcing a universal genie rule that stipulates that Jeannie has to find a temporary master, otherwise she is doomed to leave earth and Major Nelson forever.

Ken Kercheval, who played Cliff Barnes in *Dallas,* plays a schoolteacher whom Jeannie enlists to help her in her quest. Jeannie encounters a myriad of obstacles, including having to negotiate life in the singles scene, 1990s-style.

The thought of reprising a role I'd played twenty-five years before was pretty scary, and I was tentative about accepting it. For one thing, I was sure that the audiences would expect me to have exercised a brand of magic and still look the same. After some deliberation, I decided not to allow vanity to get the better of me. Although Jeannie was not my alter ego, I was still deeply attached to her, and, after a great deal more soul-searching, I took the part. I never regretted it.

It must also be said that in the years since *I Dream of Jeannie* was first on the air, and despite the myriad of roles I'd played since then, it was virtually impossible for me to shake the ghost of Jeannie, even if I'd wanted to.

Here's a classic, if unpleasant, example: in 1991, I made a TV movie, *Her Wicked Ways,* in which I played a White House reporter. Heather Locklear also played a reporter. She was lovely and great to work with, but her husband, Tommy Lee, was quite another story.

We were on location in Washington, D.C., when in the middle of the night, the phone rang. I said hello, and heard Tommy Lee's voice.

TOMMY: "Oh, my! I'm looking for my wife. Where is she?"

ME: "I don't know. You must have dialed the wrong number."

TOMMY: "Well, who am I talking to, then?"

ME: "You're talking to Barbara."

TOMMY: "Well, hello, Barbara. You wouldn't know Heather's room number, would you, darling?"

ME, MY VOICE DRIPPING WITH FROST: "Sorry, I don't. Goodbye."

TOMMY: "Don't hang up on me, honey, now, don't." [Clinking of glasses from the other end of the line] "Hey, guys! Guess what! I've got Jeannie on the phone! I've got Jeannie on the phone!"

The resultant roar that came across the line almost deafened me.

I cut off the call, left the receiver on the night table, curled up in bed again, and did my best to fall asleep.

Dreams of Jeannie? Now and again it was a nightmare.

Had I truly wanted to escape my *I Dream of Jeannie* legacy (and I did not), the rerelease of the series on Nick at Night in 1994 would have made it impossible. My picture was plastered the length and breadth of a building on Sunset Boulevard in Los Angeles and on a building in the middle of Times Square in Manhattan. I happened to be in New York City that week and had no idea about the publicity campaign, so you can imagine my shock when my cab drove through Times Square and I looked up to see myself many times larger than life!

The year before, I'd made two NBC movies set in San Francisco, the first of which was entitled *Visions of Murder,* in which I played Dr. Jesse Newman, a psychologist who works in the San Francisco police department and has psychic abilities. The handsome and distinguished actor James Brolin, who is now married to Barbra Streisand, played my first husband. In the sequel, another actor took that role. I was sorry about that, as James is a very nice, steady man and a good actor.

Speaking of Barbra Streisand, when I was making *The Confession* with Elliott Gould, Barbra was starring in *Funny Girl* on Broadway. Elliott was extremely affable and was kind enough to take me to see the show (which was incredible, and her legendary performance spectacular), and afterward he took me backstage to meet Barbra. She was extremely down-to-earth, and not a little discomfited when Shirley MacLaine arrived backstage and showered her with compliments. After Shirley left, Barbra turned to me and said, "She's a big star, isn't she? So what's with the big red nails?" So refreshing, and very real.

When I made *Visions of Murder,* I was hopeful that Dr. Jesse Newman might develop into a Jessica Fletcher–type character, with the same resonance and long-term success that Angela Lansbury achieved with *Murder, She Wrote.* The producers were probably thinking along the same lines, but after the second movie, that didn't come to fruition.

However, I did enjoy working in San Francisco again, and relished the coincidence of my playing a psychic in the same city where I had consulted Emma Nelson Sims, whose psychic predictions about me proved to be so uncannily accurate.

Unfortunately, while making *Visions of Murder* and the sequel,

Eyes of Terror, I couldn't find Emma, though I'd have relished her input. Instead, in the interest of accurately portraying a psychic, I consulted psychic Sylvia Browne.

Like my character, Dr. Jesse Newman, Sylvia also worked with the San Francisco Police Department on solving cases, and had a high success rate in doing so. When we got to know each other better, she confided in me that she found her work, which she did pro bono, extremely painful, particularly when missing children she was seeking turned up dead. But there were physical issues for herself, too.

A case in point: She was investigating the abduction and murder of a child when all of a sudden she felt blows all over her body and was bruised, just as the child had been. She then had a vision of the child's abductor, which, when he was caught, proved to be accurate. I was so impressed that I partially based my portrayal of Jesse on Sylvia.

In 1996, I also made *Dead Man's Island,* in which I played an investigative journalist, Henrietta O'Dwyer Collins. I owned the rights to the book on which the movie was based, and co-starred in it with Morgan Fairchild and William Shatner. For some reason, in those days before *Boston Legal* and remembering William's role as Captain Kirk, I expected him to be staid and stuffy. Boy, was I in for a surprise!

During the five-week shoot, he proved to be a lot of fun. In one scene, he had to wear a one-piece swimsuit and was supposed to swim in a large pool, then get out, dripping wet, and stroll down a path while simultaneously conducting a conversation with Roddy McDowall. Well, William was quite heavy at the time, and the swimsuit that wardrobe had selected for him was a 1920s-style getup. In addition, wardrobe gave him a rubber bathing cap to wear that was extremely tight. But gallant and self-deprecating William Shatner just laughed his way through the scene, making fun of the outfit and, above all, of himself. A great sport and such good company!

*   *   *

My friends always say that I am all work and no play. They are sometimes right, but now and again I do indulge my love for exotic adventure travel. And so I was thrilled when I was invited to attend the Silver Jubilee of King Hassan II of Morocco (otherwise known as the "Finger of God on Earth"), along with Michael York and Robert Stack; the head of Atlantic Records, Ahmet Ertegun; and Ahmet's wife, Mica.

We were flown first-class to Marrakech, where the streets were lined with orange blossom trees and floodlit in red, green, and orange lights, the colors of the Moroccan flag. The celebrations centered around the king's fifteenth-century palace in Marrakech, and no expense was spared in making them spectacular beyond belief.

Before the trip, I'd been warned not to wear anything that revealed my arms or my legs. I brought a glamorous long white gown with cap sleeves, completely forgetting that the gown had a low-cut neckline and a slit up the front of it. With it I wore a white fox stole.

When the escort arrived at our hotel to drive us to the castle, she took one look at me and screamed, "Oh la la!"

"Oh la la?" I said.

Recovering her composure, she explained that I had to wear something else that evening. Good idea—except that this was the only long gown I'd brought with me, and I told her so.

Her solution? She took my white fox stole and draped it

diagonally across my body, so that it covered one arm and one leg. Then she pressed my left arm across my chest and my right across my legs. Difficult to imagine, I suppose, but I hope you get the picture.

"Stay that way!" she instructed.

So I did, teetering to the car in my four-inch heels, my arms, legs, and fox fur all in place.

Once we arrived at the immense palace courtyard, I kept myself covered as best I could and watched enthralled as the king rode a black stallion the whole length of the courtyard and thousands of Berbers in white djellabas bowed down before him and wished him a long life.

Then we were escorted inside the palace, which was furnished with bizarre reproduction Victorian furniture, and into an ante-room, where a group of women, all dressed in long dresses cinched by heavy gold belts, chattered away like a flock of starlings. Although we were all girls together now, as it were, I still kept my arms strategically placed across my body and made sure that my fox fur didn't slip from its designated position.

Then a ripple of excitement shot through the anteroom.

"The king, the king is coming!" the women cried.

"Remember, you don't offer to shake hands with the king unless he offers his first," my escort instructed me.

As I was holding my arms over my chest to cover it, and wished I had some Krazy Glue to fix them there, I was relieved.

Too soon, of course, because the moment the king came into view, the first person he approached was me. And the first thing he did was offer me his hand in greeting. And who was I not to take it?

Fortunately, the king kept his eyes focused firmly on my face, and I breathed a silent sigh of relief.

Afterward, we were led out to a huge garden, bigger than a

football field, where the ground was covered by precious Persian carpets, each sprinkled with rose petals.

No alcohol was served, but there were massive tables, many piled high with all manner of sweets, including slivered almonds, hard candy, and petits fours. Groups of wrinkled old men made mint tea for all the guests.

The following day, we had lunch at La Mamounia, Winston Churchill's favorite hotel, which had beautiful rows of orange trees in the gardens. There we were served cold lobster, chicken galantine, and shrimp-stuffed artichokes. Again, the ground was laid with Oriental carpets sprinkled with rose petals.

The fête was rounded out by folk dancing, visits to the souks, and further exhibitions of horsemanship. All breathtaking, and opulent in the extreme. I was amazed to discover that the king had no fewer than ten thousand retainers to serve his every need!

* * *

I was happy living the single life and had no expectations of ever finding love again. Then one morning my friend Marilyn called out of the blue and announced, "Barbara, I met somebody last night. He's really cute, and I like him. Do you want to date him?"

As usual, all I was doing was working, and the prospect of a date was enticing. The problem was, I simply didn't have time, so I sighed and regretfully told Marilyn so. But she was having none of it; to her credit, she convinced me to set aside a weekend night on which to meet this new man she was touting so highly.

I was in my fifties and didn't dream that I would ever fall in love again, but I was willing to meet Marilyn's cute new acquaintance. So I was pleased when, a few weeks later, I received a call from Jon

Eicholtz. I immediately liked the sound of his voice, his Texas accent, and the decisive yet courteous way in which he suggested that it might be more relaxing if we didn't double-date with Marilyn and her husband but went out to dinner alone at Morton's so that we could really get to know each other.

The first thing that impressed me about Jon, apart from his perfect manners, was that he had never seen a single episode of *I Dream of Jeannie* and wasn't remotely starstruck. Quite a relief, especially after Chuck. Like Chuck, he was born in Chicago, but I decided not to hold that against him.

And I was relieved that he had nothing whatsoever to do with show business. His father had been in the army during World War II, and Jon went to the University of Kansas. Now a builder/developer, he had a five-year degree in architectural engineering. Like me, he had a twenty-six-year-old son; he had been married twice, and was now a widower.

Soon after we met, I consulted one of my doctors, and incidentally learned that he had referred Jon's wife Jeanine to a specialist after she was diagnosed with breast cancer. In the process, he grew to know Jon very well. In fact, when I told him I was dating Jon, he said, "Be good to him. I've seen a lot of husbands when their wives were ill and dying, and most of them usually run for the hills because they can't stand it, but Jon was there with her every minute. He'd wash her hair, bring her meals, and was so good to her."

On that first date, I quickly realized that Jon was so straightforward, so solid, and so dependable that next to him, I felt lightweight and frivolous. As a result, I assumed that he wouldn't like me at all. But I gave the date my best shot, and we spent most of the evening talking about his work, which was interesting. At the end of the evening, he took me home and made no attempt to kiss me goodnight, so I guessed that I'd never hear from him again.

But I was wrong. He called and we went out on a second date together, then a third. Generally, it takes me several dates with a man before I sense that romance is on the horizon, bells start to ring, and my heart begins to melt. And while I'd love to say that meeting Jon was like a thunderbolt, that I fell in love with him at first sight, that wouldn't be the truth.

We had a few more dates—romantic candlelight dinners, kisses under the stars, heart-to-heart talks, confidences exchanged, closeness established—but the moment when I knew I'd fallen in love with him now and forever was far less conventional.

We'd been invited to a Christmas party, but I was doing some night filming at the studio, and Jon came there to get me. He'd never been on a film set before, but instead of being dazzled and in awe, I could tell he was curious and, being an extremely neat and tidy man, not a little discomfited by all the on-set chaos.

He was wearing a three-piece suit and looked entirely out of place with all the crew and the actors. As he walked across the set, picking his way carefully over the cables, observing all the disarray around him, he seemed like a stranger just arrived in another world, a world where he was uncomfortable but not intimidated. A fish out of water, I guess, much in the same way as Jeannie was.

I offered him a chair, but he shook his head and instead stood and surveyed the surrounding scene with mounting disbelief.

At that point, the director started to move a big table, all on his own. As Jon watched him struggling, he turned to the crew, who were hanging around, and said, "Hey, you guys, can't somebody help him move the table?"

No one moved, and Jon looked at me questioningly.

"They can't help him," I explained. "Only the props guys can. It's a union issue, and those guys are camera crew, so their union categorically bans them from moving furniture."

Jon thought that was ridiculous and was really upset about what he considered the unfairness of the situation. And it was at that moment that I started to fall in love with him.

Then we went on a romantic trip to Egypt together, and my love for Jon intensified even more. After that, he took me to Paris, where he introduced me to his late wife's family, with whom he is very close. In a way, Egypt and Paris turned out to be our advance honeymoon.

Jon and I decided to be married at Grace Cathedral, in San Francisco, one of the most beautiful churches in the country, and world-renowned for its two sacred labyrinths—one in the forecourt and the other in the cathedral itself.

However, Jon and I picked Grace Cathedral primarily because of my personal connections to it. It was at Grace Cathedral where I was baptized and confirmed in the Episcopal Church, and I went to Sunday school there.

Before we could set the date, cathedral officials informed us that we had to meet with the priest there. On the appointed day, we were shown into his presence, and I told him all about my links with the cathedral. He was pleased, but then he sprang a not-too-pleasant surprise on us. According to Grace Cathedral protocol, he explained, since both Jon and I had been married before to other people, we were obliged to go to our respective churches in Southern California and get the ministers to send him letters recommending us.

Jon and I exchanged worried glances, as neither of us belonged to a church near our respective homes there. Then I remembered that I'd gone to Easter services at a church near my home in Beverly Hills, and that that church was run by a very avant-garde minister. So Jon and I hastily made an appointment to see him, planning to tell him about the required letter of recommendation and throwing ourselves on his mercy in the hope that he would write it for us. That meeting went very well, and we were told that the next required step was for us to see another minister, who would instruct us in the finer points of the religion.

Beforehand, we were both nervous, not knowing what he was going to ask us. In particular, Jon was worried that he might ask us about sex, and if we were sleeping together.

Seeing how worried he was, I reassured him. "No, no, definitely not, Jon. A man of the cloth would never ask that question!"

Jon was mollified, and I breathed a sigh of relief. So we set off together for Grace Cathedral and our appointment with the third minister.

First he asked us about our individual attitudes toward marriage, then about our respective children, our relationships with them, and how the children felt about each of us. Then he asked another question: "Well, then, how's sex? Are you sleeping together?"

I nearly jumped out of my skin. Finally I mumbled, "Yes," then held my breath, half expecting to be hit by a thunderbolt.

"Right, that's good," the minister said.

Jon and I breathed a collective sigh of relief and thanked our lucky stars to have found a nonjudgmental minister.

Once we'd gotten the letter we needed, we rushed home and called our friends, asking them to come to the wedding and then to the Fairmont for champagne and cake in the suite we had rented for our wedding night.

Our wedding invitation was so impromptu, so last-minute, that when I arrived at the cathedral, I half expected none of our friends to have turned up at all. Boy, was I in for a big surprise! The church was full, and all our friends were on hand to witness our wedding.

In the midst of greeting all our friends, there was a hilarious moment when a good-looking young man in purple priest's garb came up behind Jon and his son, Jon David, and hollered, "Hey, Jon?" Jon

David spun around and said, "Lucky Chuckie?" It turned out that the two of them had gone to college together at SMU in Texas!

Jon and I walked down the aisle together, hand in hand. My sister, Alison, stood up for me, and Jon David stood up for Jon. The ceremony was moving, the reception afterward warm and congenial. The day would have been perfect, except for one thing. Amid all our happiness, all our joy, all the love and the hopes for our future, one person was missing from our joyous wedding—my son, Matthew.

But Matthew's absence from my wedding was neither a surprise nor a snub. He was in residence at the Hazelden Clinic in Minnesota, one of the eight times the clinic would make another attempt to cure him of his drug addiction, an addiction that dated back to when he was just ten years old.

✴ ✴ ✴ ✴ ✴ ✴ *chapter 13* ✴ ✴ ✴ ✴ ✴ ✴

THE END

✴ ✴ ✴ ✴ ✴ ✴ ✴ ✴ ✴ ✴ ✴ ✴ ✴ ✴ ✴ ✴

IN HINDSIGHT, THE signposts are so clear, the pitfalls so evident, Matthew's fate so inevitable, but living through the hell of all of it, day by day, week by week, year by year, was quite another story. And it is really only now that I've finally been able to look back and piece together the full, horrifying saga of my son's tragic descent into drug addiction.

In 1974, Michael, Matthew, and I were living in our ranch-style home in the San Fernando Valley, a prosperous community of well-heeled, well-educated people. Little did we know that someone who lived close by, a wealthy hippie, a man with children of his own, was growing pot in his garden and smoking it with the neighborhood kids. I guess that particular person thought that what he was doing was fun, cool, harmless. If I ever came face-to-face with him, I'd happily kill him.

Fate is so strange, and I often ask myself this question: if Michael and I had lived in another neighborhood, not one where our neighbor was growing pot and handing it out to kids like some kind of candy, would Matthew have avoided becoming a drug addict?

But the reality may well be different. Marijuana can be an extremely addictive drug, and the addiction is intensified if a child not only starts smoking when he is extremely young but also has a marked genetic predisposition to addiction. Sadly, Matthew fell into both categories. Michael and I both had alcoholism in our respective families. Michael's grandfather was an alcoholic, as were both my mother's older sister and her brother. Matthew's early addiction to marijuana easily led to an addiction to harder drugs later on.

Another factor, one for which I will blame myself to my dying day, is that Matthew was only nine when I asked Michael for a divorce, and he never really recovered from having his hitherto happy home broken up. He wanted his mommy and daddy to stay together forever, but I denied him that, and will feel guilty about that for the rest of my life. If I were able to turn back the clock, I would have stayed married to Michael until Matthew was older and able to cope with us splitting. To be fair to myself, the majority of kids from broken homes don't use drugs, but that still doesn't console me.

At the time of my divorce from Michael, I never dreamed of the impact our divorce would have on Matthew. As the years flew by, he seemed like a happy little boy, albeit one who slept a little longer than most kids his age, but drugs? Never!

It wasn't as if Michael and I were neglectful or permissive parents. Quite the reverse. I had always made it my business to check out as much as I could about the children with whom Matthew played, and I made sure to visit their homes to ascertain that everything there was all right and that it was safe for Matthew to visit. Of course, I didn't know what a marijuana bush looked like.

Looking back, I see that one of the main problems is the manner in which I was raised, which discouraged me from looking into Matthew's drawers or snooping in his closet. How wrong I was. And if I could live my life again, I would look in Matthew's drawers and snoop in his closet, simply because it is dangerous not to. After all, I was the parent, I was the responsible adult, and I should have made it my business to check on Matthew at every turn. Instead, I carried on, oblivious.

Despite my short foray into the world of party drugs with Chuck, I was basically ignorant about drugs and addictive behavior. For years, the Doors' anthem "Light My Fire" had been one of the highlights of my Las Vegas act. It was only after Matthew explained it to me that I realized that the lyrics referred to marijuana.

Neither Michael nor I had recognized the signs of serious drug addiction in Matthew: the weight loss, the sluggishness, the inexplicable bouts of temper, the hours wasted in sleep, the dramatic personality changes. The trouble was that, like many parents, Michael and I were still living partly in the past, warm and secure in our glowing memories of the adorable child who loved both of us and whom we both loved so much. But when it comes to drugs, as we would learn during the harsh years that followed, love just isn't enough. Neither Michael nor I had the slightest intimation that our beloved Matthew was secretly taking drugs, spending his nights and days in his room doing little else.

The truth only slowly began to dawn on me in 1984. Matthew was nineteen and studying at City College in the San Fernando Valley. Each morning I watched proudly as he set off for college, his books in hand, eager to start a day of studying, or so I fondly imagined.

One day I came into the kitchen to find that he'd left all his schoolbooks on the counter. I grabbed them, got in the car, and raced to City College as fast I could, hoping against hope that I'd get the books to Matthew before his first class of the day began.

I looked all over for him, then, in desperation, went to the administrator's office and explained, "I have to find Matthew Ansara. He left his schoolbooks at home, and I have them for him, so please could you direct me to his classroom?"

The administrator shook her head. "I'm sorry, we don't have a Matthew Ansara at this college," she said.

Outraged at her inefficiency, I demanded that she check again. Same answer. Matthew was not registered at City College, nor had he ever been.

Despondent and afraid, I drove home and waited there for him, trembling from head to foot with a combination of fear and anger.

When Matthew arrived, I confronted him directly about not going to college, about baldly lying to me and pretending he was. Thereupon Matthew, generally a sweet and kind boy, flew into a vicious rage. There was no explanation, no excuse, no apology, not even a glimmer of contrition. Then he stomped off into the night.

I immediately jumped to the conclusion that he had gone to Michael's house. But I didn't hear a word from either Matthew or Michael. Distraught with worry, I finally called Michael, who, shocked beyond measure, told me that Matthew had not come home, nor had he heard from him for quite a few days.

We spent the next days searching for Matthew all over town, in bars, even under the freeway. For a hellish month we called friend after friend, to no avail. Neither of us had a clue where our son was living, whom he was with. Eventually we were able to discover that Matthew had been living partly on the streets and partly with a friend who'd taken him in out of pity.

Not long afterward, I received the call that helped rip the last vestiges of the veil of ignorance from my eyes. An off-duty officer called me to say that he had Matthew in custody and that he shouldn't be driving a vehicle because he was dangerous both to himself and to other people.

My then-boyfriend, Stanley Frileck, and I jumped into our cars and drove up to Mulholland Drive, where we met the police officer, who still had Matthew with him.

Before we drove off, me in my car and Stanley driving Matthew in his, the officer wagged his finger at me and said, "You'd better find out what your son's been taking!"

A further shock was ahead of me when Matthew had an almost fatal accident while driving a truck. He totaled the truck, broke his nose, and cracked a clavicle. At that point, Michael and I joined forces and confronted him.

Faced by both of us, and put under the greatest possible pressure we could muster, he would only admit, "All I do is a little pot and a pill or two. Everybody does exactly the same, Mom!"

"I don't give a flying fig if everybody does it," I said. "Drugs are unhealthy and taking them is against the law."

Looking back, I can't help seeing how naive I was. Did I really think that if I, his adoring mother, read him the riot act and gave him a civic lecture about the illegality of drugs and the ill effects of using them, my son would stop taking them altogether? Yes, and pigs would have flown to the moon.

In the end, Matthew agreed to go into rehab, and Michael and I thought the worst was over. After a few days, we were summoned to see the drug counselor, who, without making any bones about it, handed us a lengthy list of all the drugs Matthew had been taking on a regular basis.

Electrified, Matthew lunged for the list and screamed, "Don't hurt my mom and dad! I don't want them to know anything about what I've been doing."

It was too late. We read the list. We didn't want to believe it, but he had been using practically every hard drug in the world, and not in small quantities, either.

I started crying.

Matt promised to kick the habit, and I believed him. But the story had only just begun, although I didn't know it at the time. (If I had, I think I'd have gone crazy.)

Over the next few years, Matthew fought against his drug habit, but with little success. Although Michael and I were divorced, we were united in our burning desire that Matthew be cured, and we prayed each night that he'd succeed in banishing drugs from his life.

Meanwhile, I tried every conceivable way of helping him in his battle: maternal love, tough love, Al-Anon. One of the hardest lessons came after he'd attended yet another rehab. The counselor explained to us that if a child is using drugs, he has become the drugs; he is no longer your child and he no longer has a home with you. I found out Matthew was still using, and I locked him out of the house.

Over a period of fourteen years, Matthew was in and out of drug rehab constantly. And each time I went through the same process, rather like a sleepwalker following the same steps over and over.

When he left for rehab, I'd stand there crying, praying, *Dear God, please let this work. He's a good boy—let him lick this addiction before it destroys him.* Then the waiting began, battling the fears and rejoicing in the hope that this time he would come out cured and start his life again, for real and for always.

After I met Jon, he became the greatest support possible to me during all the vicissitudes of Matthew's struggle with drugs. We'd just begun our relationship when I went to visit Matt in Hazelden. Like I'd done many times before, I flew to Minnesota by myself and checked into a hotel. I saw Matthew at the clinic, spent time with him there, and spoke with his counselors, then flew back to LA a few days later.

This time when I got back to my hotel near Hazelden, the

manager greeted me with the words "Your friend is very worried about you!" and handed me a sheaf of messages from Jon. I called him immediately, happy because I finally had someone in my life who cared about me. I wasn't accustomed to that anymore, and I loved and gloried in it.

By the time Matthew was in his twenties, I'd learned the cruel and bitter lesson that no matter how much I loved him, it was fool-hardy to fall into the treacherous trap of trusting him. Although I longed for his visits and enjoyed every moment of them, after he left I would be confronted with harsh reality: silverware was missing, and often money from Jon's wallet. Matthew became almost brazen about how he stole from us in order to fund his drug habit, announcing, "Here I am, better lock up everything in the house!"

But when he was sober, he'd tell me, "I'm so sorry, Mom. I love you more than anyone else in the world."

I believe he did. But drugs held more power over him. There were some hopeful times, but they rarely lasted. When he was twenty-seven, he fell in love with a marvelous woman, an accountant, and they had a big, glamorous wedding in Oregon. I was so proud and happy, particularly afterward when he got a job and began studying creative writing at UCLA part-time. Then the cycle began again.

Heroin became both his master and his mistress. His wife couldn't take it anymore and, understandably, left him, though she didn't stop caring about him.

One night, just after her separation from him, I received a call from Matthew. He sounded half dead and managed to moan, "Please help me, Mom, I'm sick, I'm really sick."

Dolores and I, and Michael's wife, Beverly, swung into action. Together we raced to Matthew's apartment in Venice, which I'd rented for him in the hope that he would create a new and healthier life for himself there.

By the time we got to the apartment, Matthew was unconscious, clearly having overdosed. Terrified out of our wits, the three of us carried him out to the car and rushed him to the hospital. I was worried to death about him, but I was also as mad as hell. I'd been paying the rent at the apartment, but it was filthy. There were no sheets on the bed, and cartons of old food were moldering on the floor. He was hooked on heroin again, and there was nothing on God's earth that I could do about it.

When he was twenty-nine, Matthew was diagnosed with clinical depression and given medication, but that didn't help him. He still couldn't keep a job and couldn't stay in school, and he was still hopelessly hooked on heroin.

In 1999, however, he took part in a documentary about me, in which he talked about me in loving terms and at the same time chose to go public with his drug addiction. It was deeply moving, but no guarantee that he'd banished drugs from his life forever.

In 2000, though, hope flared again when he got clean and became engaged to a wonderful girl, Leanna Green. He and Leanna moved into an apartment in Covina together, and my son's life seemed to be back on track again. To be honest, "again" didn't really enter into it, because since the age of ten the only track Matthew had been on was one utterly dominated by drugs.

Recently he had been devoting himself to bodybuilding. He was six foot four and he'd bulked up to 280 pounds, determined to win the Mr. Muscle competition in Los Angeles that July. Better still, he had a small part as an inmate in an upcoming prison thriller, *Con Games.* He was so proud that he had gotten the job based on his own talent and that he had never told anybody who his parents were.

He and I were closer than ever, and he visited me and Jon several times a week. One day he told me, "Life is great, Mom. I can't believe I spent so many years not being awake to how green the trees are."

*

Initially I was almost afraid to allow myself to experience even a modicum of joy and optimism about Matthew's future. Realizing that my feelings wouldn't influence the outcome of his struggle with drugs, either positively or negatively, I decided to throw caution to the wind and flung myself into preparations for my son's wedding. I even caught myself thinking of names for my grandchildren.

The call came at 3:00 AM on June 26, 2001. For the past fourteen years, whenever my telephone rang, I had consistently feared the worst: news that Matthew was injured or dead. During that time I lived on a precipice of fear, just waiting for the inevitable to happen, yet always escaping the final drop.

But on the morning of June 26, all my worst fears came true. Matthew was dead.

I heard the news from Michael's cousin. Although Matthew always carried a note in his pocket with my name and phone number on it, the police didn't want to call me directly and tell me what had happened. I later found out that the authorities always call a close relative to break the news of a child's death to that child's parent.

He'd been found at nine the previous evening, his body slumped over the steering wheel of his truck at a Chevron gas station in Monrovia, near the 210 freeway. He was alone, and there was no evidence of trauma or foul play.

The press reported that twenty-five paramedics were called to the scene. It didn't matter how many there were; it was too late. Beside Matthew's body, they found a syringe as well as vials of anabolic steroids; he'd been injecting himself to bulk up for the bodybuilding contest. Blood tests revealed that he had shot up with a dose of unusually pure heroin, which had proved too much for his heart.

Matthew was buried at Forest Lawn Memorial Park. He was just thirty-five years old.

*

*   *   *

Sometimes I come across a photograph of myself at Matthew's funeral, looking drawn, thin, and tired beyond belief. When I was a child and then a teenager and upset about something, my mother would always say, "Remember, Barbara, no one has died! That's the only thing that's important. No one has died. Put it into perspective."

Now Matthew—young, vital, and loving—had died, and that was the only thing that was important. I wanted to die myself, but I remembered what Matthew had once said about me on a TV show: *My mother is one of the strongest people I've ever met.* Once upon a time, maybe, but not now, not now that he had gone. But I remembered what he'd said, and I knew it would be disrespectful to Matthew if I couldn't be strong.

In the days, weeks, months, and years since the funeral, I have put one foot in front of the other and carried on as best as I could. In the intervening years, I've often been asked how anyone can cope with losing a child, and the answer is that you don't. You can't. There's no way. You don't know how you will live through it, how you can survive. But you just do. There's no other choice.

I can still laugh, I can still go to parties, I can still have fun, but there's a part of me that is missing and always will be. Matthew is never out of my mind, and the pain of losing him and of missing him doesn't get less. Not on his birthday, not on Christmas, not on my birthday. Never. But he's always with me. I talk to him constantly, and I will miss him forever.

* * * * * * chapter 14 * * * * * *

IT'S A WRAP

* * * * * * * * * * * * * * *

SINCE MATTHEW'S DEATH, I've gone public about his battle with drugs during an hour-long live interview with Larry King, and I also gave an interview to *Good Morning America* during which I—who never cry in public—broke down in floods of tears on camera, in front of a nationwide audience of millions.

But no matter how severe the pain of reliving Matthew's death and his struggle against drugs, it is worth it to me if, through my openness, I am able to help just one parent spot in their child the early signs of drug addiction that I failed to recognize in Matthew.

As I write this, nine years have passed since his death, and I still think of him every day and dream of him every night. I am so blessed that through it all Jon was always by my side.

* * *

Today, happily, my career continues to keep me busy in a variety of new and challenging roles. I still think of *I Dream of Jeannie* with great affection, and greatly appreciate the opportunities it has brought me through the years. The show has proved very popular over the years, and luckily, some of that popularity has rubbed off on me. I became a spokesperson for L'eggs panty hose, and appeared in commercials for Old Navy, TV Land, and Guarantee Trust Life Insurance. Great fun was a commercial for the RX 300 Lexus in which I'm wearing my *I Dream of Jeannie* harem costume and sitting in the back of the car. All fun, and nicely lucrative for me; I was happy to do them.

I was invited to the Aladdin Resort and Casino in Las Vegas to celebrate the thirty-fifth anniversary of *I Dream of Jeannie* and to unveil the latest Barbie doll: an exact replica of Jeannie. Dressed in a pink harem outfit, complete with a pink veil, the Jeannie Barbie doll comes with crossed arms, and looks as if she is about to blink at any second.

A glitzy *I Dream of Jeannie* slot machine featuring a logo of me as Jeannie, dressed in her trademark harem pants and skimpy top, was launched in casinos throughout America. In a cute technical trick, the machine played a tape of my voice purring at players, "Oh, that's wonderful, Master," or "Yes, Master! Yes! Yes!" when they won, or "Back in the bottle! Try again" when they lost.

One day my dear friend and hairdresser Zak Taylor and I were at Donald Trump's Taj Mahal in Atlantic City when I must have been inspired by the spirit of Jeannie's evil twin sister. We were walking through the casino when I heard my voice say, "Yes, Master," and saw a young man playing the *I Dream of Jeannie* slot machine. I crept up behind him and, just as he was about to pull the handle, whispered, "May I help you, Master? I will do that for you, Master!" He almost fell off his stool, and Zak and I nearly died laughing. But we ended up paying a price for having been so mischievous, as crowds of people immediately gathered around me and I ended up spending the rest of the evening signing autographs.

There are still Jeannie machines in casinos all over America. There are Jeannie board games. There's even a Jeannie porn film! Who would have imagined that when the series first came out? The show and I were supposed to be so innocent—the censors actually banned me from revealing my belly button on TV!

I've been fortunate to have many memorable moments in my career: a star on the Hollywood Walk of Fame, a round-the-world USO tour with Bob Hope during the first Gulf War (Bob referred to the tour as the "Persian Gulp"). I was most honored to be invited by President George W. Bush to be mistress of ceremonies at a White House Christmas tree lighting ceremony, which took place outside in front of an audience of six thousand people, and to be invited to have dinner at the White House afterward.

It was snowing heavily when I arrived at the White House, and all the seats had to be wiped clean for the audience. As a dyed-in-the-wool California girl, I thought the event would have to be canceled. But parents arrived with their eager-faced children, and the ceremony went on as planned. President and Mrs. Bush arrived to watch and stayed in their box for the entire event. I sang several Christmas carols, ending with the perennial favorite "Have Yourself a Merry Little Christmas." Then Santa, played by country-and-western singer Roy Clark, made his entrance onstage.

I introduced him to the audience, then left the stage and headed for the dressing room. Before I got very far, the director rushed up to me.

"Barbara! Go back onstage again! Santa has lost his pants! Get out there and pull them up for him," he said.

"Forget it," I said. "There's no way I'm going to touch Santa's pants!"

I peeked through the curtains just in time to see Santa finish his song with his pants right down below his knees. I went back onstage again and thanked him for being on the show, but all the time I kept my eyes fixed firmly on his face!

In 2006, Larry and I reunited in a stage production of A. R. Gurney's wonderful two-person play *Love Letters*. Romantic, nostalgic, sentimental, a bittersweet commentary on the passing of time and the changing face of love through the decades, the play was the perfect vehicle for us. As always, working with Larry was a delight.

There is excited talk at Sony these days about a big-screen feature film of *I Dream of Jeannie,* with stars like Cameron Diaz, Jessica Simpson, Alicia Silverstone, and even Gwyneth Paltrow being considered to play Jeannie. My dear friend Sid Ganis, a producer who recently completed two terms as president of the Academy of Motion Picture Arts and Sciences, has been shepherding the project for quite a while now, and has never lost faith in the property. When it's made, I'd like to be around to see it. Sidney Sheldon always said that one day he wanted to see me play Jeannie's mother. Perhaps, perhaps not. All I know is that I intend to be working until I'm ninety.

Jon and I continue to live in our Beverly Hills home, along with our Labradoodle, Djinn Djinn, named after the dog in *I Dream of Jeannie.*

The wonderful thing about my business and about my life is that I never know what's around the corner. I'm very lucky to like what I do and to be able to work at it so happily and for so long. I've always considered my career to be a great joy and a great gift. I love it, and long may it continue.

ACKNOWLEDGMENTS

I want to especially thank my fans, writer Wendy Leigh, my agent, Dan Strone, and the truly wonderful and talented team brought together for my memoir by my publisher, Tina Constable, and my terrific and mentoring editor, Sydny Miner, with her assistant editor, Anna Thompson.

Without the love, encouragement, and wisdom of all of you, I would never have had the courage to get out of the bottle.

With love and appreciation,
Barbara

INSERT PHOTO CREDITS

Note: Photos that are not cited here are from the author's personal collection.

INSERT 1:

p. 1: Sony Pictures Television

p. 4 (top): Photofest

p. 5 (top): CBS Television/Photofest

p. 5 (bottom): © 20th Century Fox/Photofest

p. 6 (top): © 20th Century Fox/Photofest

p. 6 (bottom): © Twentieth Century-Fox Film Corporation/Photofest

p. 7 (top): © MGM/Photofest

p. 7 (bottom): © 20th Century Fox/Photofest

p. 8 (middle): © Twentieth Century-Fox Film Corporation/Photofest

p. 8 (bottom): © Universal Pictures/Photofest

INSERT 2:

p. 1 (top): Photofest

p. 2 (top): Photofest

p. 2 (bottom): Photofest

p. 3 (top): © NBC/Photofest

p. 3 (bottom): © NBC/Photofest

p. 4 (top): © NBC/Photofest

p. 4 (bottom): © NBC/Photofest

p. 5 (top): Photofest

p. 5 (bottom): © April Fools Productions/Photofest

p. 6 (top): © NBC/Photofest

p. 6 (bottom): © National Broadcasting Company (NBC)/Photofest

INDEX

Printed in the United States
by Baker & Taylor Publisher Services